NEW BUSINESS
MODELS F O R A
NEW ECONOMY

*Remaking the Four
Businesses of Real Estate*

JOHN TUCCILLO, Ph.D., CAE

Dearborn™
Real Estate Education

While a great deal of care has been taken to provide accurate and current information, the ideas, suggestions, general principles, and conclusions presented in this text are subject to local, state, and federal laws and regulations, court cases, and any revisions of same. This publication is sold with the understanding that the publisher is not engaged in rendering legal, accounting, or other professional service. If legal advice or other expert assistance is required, the services of a competent professional person should be sought.

Senior Vice President and General Manager: Roy Lipner
Publisher & Director of Distance Learning: Evan Butterfield
Editorial Project Manager: Louise Benzer
Production Manager: Bryan Samolinski
Typesetting: Ellen Gurak
Art and Design Manager: Lucy Jenkins

Published by Dearborn™ Real Estate Education,
a division of Dearborn Financial Publishing, Inc.®
a Kaplan Professional Company
155 North Wacker Drive
Chicago, IL 60606-1719

Printed in the United States of America.

02   03   04   10   9   8   7   6   5   4   3   2   1

DEDICATION

This book is dedicated to the leaders in the
real estate industry who keep us moving forward.

Contents

Preface

Yes, there is a new economy. Despite the collapse of the new technology sector and the disappearance of the "dot-coms," there have been significant changes in the way we do business and the way the economy works. The emergence of the new economy has forced change in virtually every sector and virtually every industry.

It is a truism to say that the real estate industry has undergone significant change over the past decade. It has done so in part because the industry itself has changed and because the economy as a whole has changed. But looked at in retrospect, the magnitude of the change has been both stunning and disappointing.

It is stunning because the industry has migrated from a "mom and pop" industry of small local firms into a more modern, consolidated sector dominated by large regional firms and national franchises. From more than 100,000 companies in 1990, the industry has shrunk to fewer than 80,000 in 2002. Part of this reflects the increased cost of operating an information business in the age of technology. Because the largest change in the economy is how we treat information, the real estate business has been crucially affected by outside forces. The tools required to operate, the expectations of consumers, and the potential for new competition have all generated significant pressures that have increased the concentration of the industry.

Prior to 1990, none of this held true in the industry. There were large firms, but their competitive reach was limited in comparison with smaller firms. The tools used were equally accessible, information was available to all practitioners, and competency resided in the human being alone. The new economy has changed all that. Because of the application of technology to real estate, size has become a real advantage.

It is disappointing because the way in which the industry does business has not changed nearly as quickly as either the economy as a whole or the structure of the industry itself. Any real estate practitioner who operated in 1990 probably operates little differently today. He or she might use a wireless phone instead of the office instrument, might keep files and records on a laptop instead of a day-timer or in a file cabinet, and may communicate with clients and customers using e-mail rather than notes, but the transaction remains largely unchanged. It still requires immense amounts of people-time and paper to conduct a real estate deal, and the deal still takes weeks to move toward closing.

The failure to use technology to streamline the real estate transaction has been the most disappointing aspect of the change affecting the real estate business. Four years ago, it seemed as if the total solution to automating the real estate transaction was just around the corner. Now that solution seems as far away as ever, and may never be implemented from within the industry. It may take the entrance of new ownership from some other industries, such as banking and insurance, where settlement technology is running and has been tried and found workable.

This book is about the changes that have and have not occurred in the real estate industry as the new economy has emerged. It looks at the relationship between brokerage, sales, association management and information transmission in the real estate industry, and attempts to offer some models that will work in the context of the new economy. The reader who is involved in the industry will find here outlines of successful approaches to organizing a business in the new economy, regardless of the part of the real estate sector in which he or she operates. As the core of the book, Chapters 6 through 9, treat each of the businesses of real estate in turn and sketch the approaches I think will work for the future.

The propositions outlined in this book are a result of my reflection on the state of the real estate industry. These opinions were formed through observation and action, and as such they owe a great deal to a great many people. I would like to acknowledge the real estate firms with whom I have worked, both brokerages and vendor companies. In each engagement I have found individuals striving to find a path to success in an uncertain future and, in many cases, finding it. I would also thank the many real estate agents with whom I have been in contact, either in person or via correspondence, and the lessons they have taught me about how even a static process can be infused with imagination and innovation. My former colleagues at Tecker Associates also contributed greatly to my thinking. Working with them crystallized my 14 years of association management experience and focused them on the future. Special thanks also go to Manny Garcia of Coldwell Banker Realty Pros, Dick Ward of Fidelity National Information Solutions, and Leslie Appleton-Young of the California Association of Realtors® who thoughtfully reviewed this book and provided useful suggestions. Finally, I thank Jeanne Grainger, whose encouragement sustained me during the writing of the book.

Chapter 1

In the Land of the Blind, the One-Eyed Man is King[1]

With many dot-coms blowing up, it is now fashionable to dismiss the Internet as just another tulip mania. That Internet stocks were a classic bubble is without question. But the Internet isn't just tulips, and if you think it is, well, let's talk in five years. By then it will be clear that the Internet is a business evolution–reshaping how businesses communicate, educate and purchase materials; a social revolution–connecting people who have never been connected before; and, for both of these reasons, a strategic dilemma that we are just beginning to understand.[2]

This book is the product of both observation and experience. The observation part comes easily: My entire professional career has been spent studying different markets and different businesses. The experience part has come harder, and it has come through sometimes unpleasant, sometimes difficult, but always educational adventures with companies attempting to be

---

[1] I am grateful to Manny Garcia, of Coldwell Banker Realty Pros, for suggesting this analogy for the new economy and the real estate business. He is writing a book of the same name. I hope I'm not preempting his work.

[2] Thomas L. Friedman, "Digital Defense," *The New York Times,* July 27, 2001, p. A21.

part of the revolution that is now remolding American business. That change we are experiencing has been referred to as "the new economy," and so I will use that term throughout the book. A little later in this introduction I will attempt to define it, or at least describe what I mean whenever I use the term.

Over the past decade or so, we have been astounded by two phenomena, seemingly very different but in reality two sides of the same coin. The first has been the explosion of new business, centered on the Internet, based in new technology, and attempting to transform old ways of doing business. The second phenomenon has been the dramatic failure of so many of these new businesses, and the subsequent pall it has cast on what had been a ten-year economic expansion—the first act in what has become a full-bore economic contraction. It's easy to believe that the rise and fall of the "dot-coms" was a short and amusing digression from the long-term course of the economy, and many commentators have argued exactly that: The skyrockets went up and came down, but the business world plods along; there is no new economy.

This would be the worst lesson to take from recent corporate history. It ignores the fact that we had record numbers of new business start-ups during the course of the 1990s, and that 80 percent of all new businesses fail, whether they use advanced nanotechnologies or pencil and paper as their tools. To argue that business failure in the technology sector is proof that there is no new economy is akin to saying that the crow of the rooster causes the sun to rise.

Yet, there are lessons for the new economy that can be taken from the recent slide. The simplest one, old and trite as it may be, forms the basis for this book: *if you fail to plan, you plan to fail.* Most of the business failures that have cast a shadow on the new economy occurred either because there was no business model or because the business model was a faulty one. The purpose of this book is to describe, analyze, and apply the new types of business arrangements that real estate practitioners are using to adapt to the changes that have occurred in information technology.

The remainder of this initial chapter is devoted to three things. First, I talk about the landscape of new business and describe why it's littered with failure. This is meant as a double lesson: first, to show you some of the pitfalls to avoid, and second, to encourage you to plan your business carefully. If you are to operate successfully in the new economy, you need to look carefully at those who have failed as well as those who have thrived. The second section details the changes that have occurred in the economic and business environments that justify calling the world we live in "the new economy." Finally, there is a guide to the rest of the book and how you can use it to your own advantage.

ADVENTURES IN DOT-COM LAND

"Where and when did it all start? We will probably never really know. So many people, initiatives and speeches have fused into one... with so many laying claim to being first."

–Stefan Swanepoel

It really did sneak up on us, this new way of doing business. If comedy isn't pretty, starting a business in a changing environment is uglier than comedy. We all know the image of the technology start-up: The staff and the guiding geniuses of the firm are all under 30 (in fact, many are under 25). They dress in a way that gives "casual" a bad name and take their dogs to work. They're housed in old warehouse space, usually in the San Francisco Bay area. They play video games, pool, soccer, and Foosball *right in the office!* And they command the attention and the money of older, more staid people called "venture capitalists." These "VCs" lavish millions of dollars on vague business models that promise to make traditional businesses more efficient by using information technology. And the firm name usually ends in ".com."

We also know the arc of the business. Fueled by seemingly unlimited amounts of money, they open their doors with great fanfare, with their stories featured in *Fast Company, Business 2.0, Red Herring, Industry Standard,* and any number of other new (and now defunct) business magazines. Then, with some more money and some more publicity, the company goes public, and investors, looking to get into the next Microsoft on the ground floor, drive the price up. But like a cheap bottle rocket on the Fourth of July, the stock eventually plummets when the essentially weak nature of the company is revealed. Now the very same magazines that pumped the company, along with the traditional media, point out the nakedness of the emperor, the retirement savings of ordinary folks evaporate, and we all feel bad.

Having a pity party for ourselves is great, but essentially useless. Rather, let's look at why these new firms failed and see if there are any lessons for doing business in the new economy. There are three general reasons why technology start-ups have failed.

1. *They saw their businesses as purely technology and refused to learn anything about the industries they entered.* Ah, the arrogance of youth! There have been many tech start-ups who saw every problem as a nail simply because they knew how to use a hammer. As I will describe later, technology is a tool and unless you know what you are interested in accomplishing, the tool is irrelevant at best, useless at worst.

While it happens in all industries, real estate has been a particularly fertile ground for this type of error. It is a business where local connections and human interactions make success happen. Many parts of the transaction process, however, can be automated and certainly have been and will be. This potential automation, and the rewards it promises, have been a source of great temptation for technology companies. They see the inefficiencies in the real estate transaction and the cash the transaction throws off, and they salivate over the profits to be made from making the system more efficient.

But success in real estate means skill in negotiating for and counseling buyers and sellers, and only then does it involve managing the transaction. Technologists have consistently failed to see this. There are two examples of how this plays out. The first is a company on whose board I served. In fact, I was their industry expert. The firm was a spin-off of a very successful provider of technology services and was run by executives from that company. The business model involved using salaried licensees and the Internet to streamline the transaction. Full listing and marketing services were offered at prices below the average commission rate, and buyer brokerage was available.

The company hit the ground with four offices in the San Francisco metropolitan area, choosing to serve the entire area from a limited number of locations. Prior to and during the roll-out, there was no effort to understand the mechanics of the real estate industry. In essence, management confused the location neutrality of information with the lack of a need for local representation and knowledge. In the end, revenue flow was insufficient to sustain the company and new investors were not forthcoming. At the last board meeting, management decided to enter another industry, again with no first-hand knowledge.

In another case, the lessons were learned in time. Zip Realty is a start-up firm that follows the salaricd-liccnsee model referenced above and described in Chapter 6. But Zip discovered by careful attention to the traditional real estate business that local touch is necessary for successful entrance into the market. Accordingly, Zip altered its business model to bring the company close to the consumer, rather than operating in a metropolitan area from a single location.

> 2. *They moved the business in the wrong direction.* When a new business begins, the owners need to decide how to allocate their capital. Essentially, for any business this is a choice between two courses. The traditional course has been to concentrate on product development and then to launch a complete offering into a well-planned area. This works in relatively static markets where immediate revenue is not an issue, a situation that has usually been the case with American business.

In the world of the new economy, there is an alternative business strategy that makes some sense. That strategy involves launching with an incomplete product in order to establish beachheads in target markets. Netscape did this with the Navigator browser and was rewarded quite handsomely for doing so.[3] The

---

[3] See John Tuccillo, *The Eight New Rules of Real Estate,* Chicago: Dearborn Financial Publishing, Inc. 1998, pp. 15-17, for the complete story of Netscape's launch.

objective here is to appropriate market share quickly to preempt any competition. For new products, this makes a great deal of sense. In fact, in the new economy, it's probably the essential strategy.

These two options are mutually exclusive unless the company has access to virtually unlimited capital. Prior to April 2000, the most appealing approach was to adopt the first strategy–perfect the product and gear up for large-scale rollout–and then hit the marketplace running after securing additional capital. Many firms have done this, and some–eBay is a prime example–have been successful in owning their markets because of intense preparation.

When the tech sector bubble burst, however, in April 2000, funding to implement the second phase disappeared and companies were caught in the middle. They had the product and the infrastructure to cover the market, but could not execute. A significant number of tech company start-up failures in late 2000 and early 2001 were caused by this market shift.

One of the major examples of this lies in the real estate industry. This was a company that developed a transaction management platform combined with a customer management system. The product was the highest quality available and developmentally far ahead of the competition. It was also linked to a multiple-listing service (MLS) software vendor to provide a channel into the real estate market. All this was built on initial funding. The plan was to field the product through a second round of funding. Unfortunately, the date was July 2000, and the market had dried up. Unable to execute, the company was forced to dissolve.

The lesson here is that strategy makes sense only in the context of the tenor of the market. It's not the team with the best talent and the best ideas that wins. The winners have to execute, as well.

    3. *They had no business model.* This is probably the saddest model of all. Take the case of Kozmo.com.[4] This was an online delivery service devoted to fulfilling any whim in-

---

[4] For a summary of the story, see "Kozmo's Crazy Cosmos Crashes," *The Industry Standard,* April 23, 2001, p. 27.

stantaneously, regardless of scope, for the urban masses. The idea sounded great, and soon, in selected cities, Kozmo's orange-clad messengers were servicing couch potatoes with videos and snacks. And Kozmo lost money on every transaction—the perfect IPO candidate. Unfortunately, Kozmo kept changing its business model, thus blurring its public identity.

It began as a free delivery service in 1998, pledging never to charge. By the end of 2000, users were placing such small orders that Kozmo introduced a delivery fee for orders below a minimum figure. Alliances with Amazon, Warner Home Video, and Starbucks were announced and never implemented successfully. As a last gasp, Kozmo attempted to publish a print catalog and shift to the phone as its communications technology, dropping the ".com" from its name. The company finally failed in April 2001.

Rivals.com suffered a similar fate. Rivals was an applications service provider (ASP) that created and administered Web sites for college sports programs and their fans. Sensing (correctly) huge market potential, Rivals initially implemented a business model that charged a small subscription fee. When this didn't produce enough revenue, it shifted its model and tried to rely on Internet advertising to sustain itself. That didn't work either, and it switched yet again to a model that sold "premium" subscriptions. Finally, it stopped the bleeding and went out of business.[5]

Not having a sure business model is one of the greatest sins of the marketplace, and the market will make you pay. If you have no model, or if your model keeps shifting, you cannot establish a brand identity with your customer base, and you will be ignored. In real estate, Homes.com and Real Estate.com had two of the best names in the business. It was clear what they were about, and consumers would flock to their sites. Yet, when you peeked behind the curtain, it was unclear what either really did. There was some Web site development, a bit of information, and some

---

[5] For a description footnote the ripples caused by Rivals collapse, see John Manasso, "Dawgvent, Border Wars Regroup After Rivals Fall," *Atlanta Journal-Constitution*, April 12, 2001, p. F2.

tools to help agents. But what was there did not add up to a clear business model. Lacking acceptance in the market, Real Estate.com failed and Homes.com split into two companies.

The fact that dot-coms have failed because of arrogance, bad luck, and stupidity is no surprise; these are the reasons behind any business failure. The beneficiaries of their failures, the firms that have picked up the assets for a song, are those who know what they don't know, time the market correctly, and pay attention to creating a strong business plan. The lesson is clear: Pay attention to the things that create winners. As you go through this book, you will see strong business models that work, how to think about the new economy and the new business environment, and how to recognize the partners you need to enlist. Put all that into the context of what has caused the failures of the dot-coms.

WHAT IS THE NEW ECONOMY?

One of the major upshots of the failures experienced over the past year has been a willingness to abandon the proposition that there is such a thing as the "new economy." The technological revolution was merely a blip in the long history of the industrial world. I'm sure that the same sentiments were expressed in 1873 when economic collapse hit the fledgling manufacturing sector. Yet, the industrial revolution in the United States was a done deal then, just as the technological revolution is a reality today.

Part of the issue is that any technological change proceeds in three stages. At first, the new technology is a toy for the rich and/or the adventurous. Then, as it seeps into general use, the technology allows us to do the same things we've always done, but differently. Finally, we use the technology to do new things. Take the internal combustion engine. We have all been exposed to the images of the first automobile users, dressed in dusters and goggles and frightening the animals—hobbyists with toys. But then we began to use the engine to pull plows and bring crops to market. Finally, the engine changed our concept of space, allowing us to build cities on highways of concrete rather than water and to build them out rather than up.

So changes occur even if we can see them, and from the ashes of failure come the seeds of real change. This book is about operating in the "new economy." and I would argue that there really is a new economy. But what exactly is it? In a recent article, Don Tapscott suggested that the characteristics of the new economy could be described as any or all of the following:

- New infrastructure for wealth creation: the Internet is the basis of economic activity
- New business models
- New sources of value: knowledge work generates value
- New ownership of wealth: equities are more widely distributed
- New educational models and institutions
- New governance[6]

The new economy can be described in the following propositions.

It Is An Economy of Abundance, Not Scarcity

The classic problem in economics is the task of reconciling unlimited wants with limited means. We can envision many things that we simply can't have because the resources needed to have them are not at our disposal. As a society, we faced this problem most clearly in the late 1970s when the oil crisis introduced us to gas lines, rationing, and an acute anxiety about vanishing resources. We no longer have those anxieties. Yes, we worry about petroleum, and water, and the environment. But the issues of scarcity are by and large of lesser concern to us than they were in the past. The reason is the new economy. It is not an economy based primarily on the transformation of things into other things. Rather, it's an economy whose primary industry is the transformation of information into knowledge.[7] Fortunately

---

[6] Don Tapscott, "Rethinking Strategy in a Networked World," *Strategy and Business,* Third Quarter, 2001, p. 38.

[7] We define "knowledge" here as actionable information. "The sun rises in the East and sets in the West" is information. "If you're lost in the woods, you can tell direction by looking at the transit of the sun" is knowledge.

(or not), the supply of information is virtually unlimited. The means that we use to create value, then, have no real limits. The economic problem now becomes one of time—how we can balance all the opportunities that the new economy presents for the creation of value.

Demographics Is The Driving Force

In open economies like the United States, demographics are always going to be the most important long-term determinant of economic activity. But this economy benefits from a demographic configuration unprecedented in the history of the United States, one that has raised the expectations of long-term prosperity to a degree also unprecedented. The major influence is, of course, the baby boom, that generation born between 1946 and 1964. Larger than any other similar group, the baby boom has determined what has happened in the U.S. economy for the past half century. Now that impact is felt in a growing, low-inflation, low-interest-rate economy. The peak year of the baby boom was 1957, which means that there are more 45-year-olds than any other single age group. Characteristically, people between the ages 40 and 50 live on the upward slopes of their lifetime productivity, income, savings, and spending curves. When you add this up across the entire society, it produces a great deal of economic activity, and that produces a bias toward prosperity.

The second major demographic change is immigration. Since 1980, the United States has welcomed in an average of 600,000 new immigrants a year. Census data suggest that the newcomers achieve an average household income equivalent to that of American families within 15 years of arrival. More importantly, within that same 15-year period, recent arrivals are much more likely to have become homeowners than are native-born Americans of similar ages. This should be no surprise. The courage it takes to pull up stakes and go to a place of which you know little is so great that rapid achievement is a simple extension. The good news for the economy is that newcomers add to growth and further bias the economy toward prosperity.

Public Policy Operates On a Rational Basis

It used to be that Washington was engaged in a tug-of-war. The Federal Reserve administered a monetary policy designed to steer the economy toward balanced, moderate growth. Meanwhile, successive Congresses and administrations sought to spend every dollar they could lay their hands on; deficit spending was a way of life. The results were tragically apparent: growing deficits, a mounting national debt, boom-bust economic cycles, and, in the later 1970s and early 1980s, double-digit inflation and interest rates.

Now, monetary and fiscal policies are much more synchronized. More importantly, for the past eight years, the mindset in Washington has shifted toward a belief in budget balancing.[8] This has meshed with the Federal Reserve's desire for long-term stability. The net result has been to reduce the role of the federal government in the economy and in financial markets. We are less a managed social welfare economy and more a market-driven economy. This has resulted in strong, consistent growth and somewhat lower interest rates. Going forward, it doesn't appear that this will change.

There Is One World Economy

In 1997 and 1998, when currency speculators brought down several of the key currencies of Southeast Asia, the American stock market plunged, a seemingly unthinkable connection.[9] How could some obscure currencies throw a shudder into the most powerful economy in the world? The answer is that there are no independent economies anymore. What happens in Thailand has repercussions in Tallahassee. That means that the state of the world economy has as great an effect on domestic events as does anything else. It also means that your business

---

[8] The budget deficits generated in the wake of the September 11, 2001, terrorist attacks and the subsequent economic recession are regarded as a departure from "business as usual."

[9] The best description of the interaction of world economies can be found in Thomas Friedman, *The Lexus and the Olive Tree,* New York: Farrar, Strauss, Giroux, 1999

plan must make explicit reference to international economic trends and flows if it is to be truly comprehensive and effective.

Technology Boosts Productivity

As you read this, think about all the tools you now use in your daily business. You probably own a cell phone and a pager, probably use a personal digital assistant or PDA, perhaps a Palm Pilot, and possibly have a laptop and a wireless modem. Most of these things were not in your tool kit five years ago, and they make you more productive. Extend that process to the entire economy, and you see how the new economy operates. Take vehicle manufacturers, as an example: In the old economy, they maintained stocks of materials so that they could keep the production line moving. The application of technology has changed all that for the better. Now, networked computers arrange for the delivery of materials just in time to be applied to production. The result is lower costs and an automatic price inflation damper.

Technology has affected information use and distribution even more dramatically. We address this as it relates to real estate in Chapter 2.

The Consumer Is King

With all these changes, the consumer has come out on top. The democratization of information has placed market power into the hands of consumers and enabled them to dictate what happens in the marketplace. We return to this point in depth in Chapter 2.

In this new economy, your most important tools are customer service and technology. The consumer is king, and businesses throughout the economy are lavishing world-class service on them. That means that consumers are constantly being educated as to what service they can expect in the marketplace. If you cannot match the levels of service presented to the market by other businesses, you are an inferior choice and will not prosper in the new economy.

Similarly, the way to deliver great customer service is to use technology wisely. The best businesses train their customer service representatives to access customer records and use them in dealing with consumers. Thus, when you call, say, Land's End to place an order, the person at the other end of the phone will be reviewing both your entire history with the company and any special sales currently in effect for items that match the items you have purchased in the past.

The image that ought to remain fixed in your mind is a kind of reverse Wizard of Oz. Only now, the folksy people person— you—is in front of the curtain and the light show is behind it. In other words, the blending of people skills and information technology should be seamless in your business and be an integral part of your business plan.

HOW TO USE THIS BOOK

This book is designed for the casual reader as well as for the reader who wants to build a new business model for the new economy. In either case, Chapters 1 through 3 are important in understanding what has occurred in the new economy, how it affects real estate, and what's important to your industry and your business. Casual readers should then follow the book in order, taking whatever lessons they wish from what's going on in real estate.

This book is divided into two sections. The next four chapters talk about the general principles that apply to the entire real estate industry in the new economy. In this section, you will learn how to think about technology, the trends that are affecting the real estate business, the competencies that are critical to your survival and profitability, and some of the tools currently available in the marketplace for your use. Every part of the industry will use these tools and needs to develop these competencies.

The next section consists of four chapters, each of which focuses on a particular business within the real estate industry and describes the business models that are currently being used by organizations in each of these businesses and the manner in which these businesses can work together. Each of these models recognizes the new economy's trends and integrates tools and competencies in an approach to the market. A final chapter ties these together.

If you are looking for new business models, the material in Chapters 6 through 9 is key. Go to the chapter that mirrors your business and look at the models that are being adopted in your line of work. Take what you need from them and consider a new way of doing business. Then loop back to Chapters 4 and 5 to look at the competencies you need to develop for success and the tools you might want to consider using.

After reading this book, you should be able to prepare a business plan (sample shown in the Appendix) to go forward in the new economy. The plan should connect the tools and competencies with the models currently being introduced to the industry. Most importantly, it should be right for you, in that it recognizes both the external reality and your particular market needs.

Chapter *2*

The New Economy and the Real Estate Industry

The new economy is not–and never was–just about dotcoms. It is not and never was just about IPOs, venture capitalists, or irrationally exuberant stock markets. It never did belong to just one industry or one part of the country.

So what is the new economy about? It is about three things: the expansion of individual opportunity, the disruptive energy of ceaseless innovation, and the transformative power of information technology and communications.[1]

Clearly, the new economy has affected all industries. Businesses have been forced to adjust the way in which they approach the market, the products and services they offer, and the way in which those products and services are priced. More importantly, both the move to the new economy and the revolution in technology that has fostered it have both caused businesses to question the conventional wisdom of what they do and how they do it. In this book we outline the results of that questioning in

---

[1] "What Is the State of the New Economy," *Fast Company,* #50 September 2001, p. 103.

the real estate industry by describing what has been done and what could be done to continue success in the midst of change.

We set the stage in this chapter by reviewing the current state of the real estate business and the impact that technology has had on it. The chapter deals with three topics. First, we look at how the information revolution has affected the real estate business. Essentially, information has become democratized, thus opening up businesses that had previously thrived as information monopolies to competition from a wide variety of sources. The material in this chapter is expanded in Chapter 3. Second, we describe how the real estate industry has evolved into four businesses and how the technological revolution has caused them to become competitors. This material is described more fully in Chapters 6 through 9. Finally, we introduce some considerations that should be taken into account when considering how to use technology. Remarkably, the best way to make a decision as to what technology to use is to not think about technology.

THE INFORMATION REVOLUTION AND REAL ESTATE

The revolution in the accumulation, interpretation, and transmission of information has dramatically affected all information-based businesses. It has done this by empowering the consumer, by giving the consumer the direct ability to inform and possibly transact business where in the past an intermediary agent was necessary. In some cases, this effect has been public and obvious. The travel agent business is the poster child here. Given the power to use the Internet to make arrangements for transportation, lodging, and other travel needs, the public has moved away from the use of agencies, devastating the industry. Research suggests that the Internet has eliminated as much as 40 percent of the agency business. While that still leaves the majority of revenues intact, it also means that large numbers of firms are gone.

Sometimes the impact is subtler and less obvious. The broadcast television networks were once the kingpins of electronic media. In the 1950s and 1960s, NBC, CBS, and ABC were large, influential corporations with significant corporate headquarters buildings in New York City. This importance derived from their monopoly position in sending pictures and sound into American homes. Their business model was very simple: We control a key distribution system and you can use it for a fee. Technological change broke this monopoly and gave viewers almost complete control over their entertainment choices. The result has been a declining viewership for the broadcast networks, reduced advertising revenues, and a decline in stature. Now, none of the three networks is an independent corporation: Disney owns ABC, Viacom owns CBS, and General Electric owns NBC. The broadcast networks are now merely parts of a broader entertainment and communications strategy.

Real estate is now in the midst of change that mirrors both the travel industry and the broadcast networks. Fundamentally, the real estate industry was been built on the control of information. The real estate agent and the real estate office were the only sources of comprehensive information on which properties were for sale and who might be interested in buying them. Any buyers or sellers who sought to realize their goals would have to come to the real estate industry. With this monopoly power, revenues were just about guaranteed. Moreover, because information was an industry monopoly (because of the shared nature of multiple-listing systems), any firm of any size could serve consumers equally well. So the number of firms grew without regard to market efficiency. Like the travel agency business, small, local firms dominated real estate.

The information revolution has changed all that. Consumers now can check on the available inventory of properties as quickly by themselves as through the agency of a real estate professional. The Internet has become the mechanism that has effectively broken the information monopoly held by the real estate industry. And the public appears to be both using the Internet enthusiastically and benefiting from it.[2]

---

[2] Right now, the Internet is a more useful tool to buyers than to sellers; listing properties on the multiple-listing system or on the Internet is still better done by an agent. However, for buyers, the evidence is clear. More than 60 percent of all home searches now begin on the Internet. A recent California Association of REALTORS® survey found that buyers who use the Internet physically see far fewer houses and buy far more quickly. More important, their overall satisfaction level with real estate professionals is higher than that of buyers not using the Internet (California Association of REALTORS®, December 2001).

Increased market leverage by the consumer is having three noticeable effects on the real estate industry. First, it has put pressure on the fees that can be charged by real estate agents. We've seen this in the proliferation of Internet-based discount firms like Zip Realty and eRealty; they offer limited services (relative to traditional firms) for a lower price. In addition, increasing numbers of agents are trying out new compensation methods such as fee-based services to adjust to the loss of an information monopoly. We describe a number of these in Chapter 7. These changes, by the way, mirror changes that are occurring in the travel agent business.

Second, the information revolution has destroyed the concept of geography. We trade financial securities around the world and around the clock. We can access information and services at any time, regardless of where in the world that information is lodged. But in the past, real estate was by necessity a geographic business. Local knowledge always figured importantly in staking out market area. If business was to be done across long distances, then contacts and referral partners who had the necessary local knowledge were used.

Now the Internet has opened all markets to all practitioners. It really doesn't matter who owns what market or who has access to local knowledge. With the Net, everyone has access to local knowledge. This both expands horizons and intensifies competition. Now you can do business with anyone anywhere just by using the resources of the Internet. It also means that anyone else in the business can compete with you in your own market areas.

The third impact of the development of information technology on real estate has been the continued consolidation of the industry. With the monopoly broken, firms have been driven to differentiate themselves through service. That requires technology, and technology requires resources. In other words, technological change has introduced economies of scale to real estate: bigger matters now. The result has been a reduction in the number of firms by about one-third in a little over a decade. We expand on the notion of the impact of technological change on the real estate business in the next chapter.

THE FOUR BUSINESSES OF REAL ESTATE

The new economy has also changed the organization of the real estate industry itself. The industry can be thought of as having both a business and an administrative side, each of which exists as an individual entity. So, we have brokers and agents as the prime business categories in the industry, but both are involved in the essentially administrative functions of the trade associations. And all three—brokers, agents, and associations— are involved in the organization of information in the multiple-listing systems (MLSs). As the industry developed on the basis of information control, all these entities seemed to be, and were regarded as, a single business.

Where these once shared common goals and were essentially the same business, technology has removed part of their value propositions and forced each to seek other models for success. In the process, the four businesses have grown apart to the point where they now pursue somewhat disparate ends. Yet, they are still linked together through market and organization structure, so the adjustments each has made have generated competition among them. (In this section, we look at the motivations now driving each of these businesses. In chapters 6 through 9, we examine in detail how each of the businesses has adapted.)

The Broker Business

The original model of the broker business centered on the recruitment and deployment of agents. Because each successful sale resulted in a commission that would be split evenly between broker and agent, the greater the number of "feet on the street," the higher the revenue for the broker. The broker was responsible for paying the majority of overhead from his share. But agents were independent contractors, so the employment expenses incurred by the broker were minimal. Well into the 1970s, the company dollar (the amount from revenue available to the broker to pay all expenses other than agent commissions) regularly exceeded 55 percent. This was more than sufficient to guarantee an acceptable profit from brokerage. And, of course, with each deal producing a substantial net, larger size meant greater profit.

It was in this environment that the franchises with which we are now familiar grew and prospered. Franchises operated with a structure similar to that of independent brokerages, except that revenues in the form of franchise fees were only indirectly derived from transactions. But the positive relationship between size and revenues was the same. Franchise membership quickly grew to become a significant feature of the industry landscape.

All this began to change with the creation of Re/Max in 1973 and the subsequent growth of the "100 percent" concept. This new franchise was focused on the agent and offered an alternative to the traditional even commission split brokers offered agents. Under the 100 percent concept, agents kept the entire commission and paid the franchisee full expenses. This model obviously reduced the company dollar received by brokers and initially appealed to high-producing agents, who saw an opportunity to increase their income by sharing less of the commission revenue with the broker.

The migration to Re/Max hurt traditional brokers in two ways. First, they lost many of their highest producers to the new franchise. While they could be replaced, the new agents were greener and thus less productive. This reduced the number of transactions and the total revenue received by the broker. Second, the presence of Re/Max caused the top producers who remained with the broker to demand higher commission splits. Brokers were forced to rethink their commission structures and in the process receive less revenue from each transaction. Eventually, every firm offered part, if not most, of its sales force the opportunity to receive the majority of the transaction commission.[3] In the past quarter century, the company dollar, the amount retained by the brokerage after commissions (and needed to pay all administrative expenses and generate profit), has fallen from more than 50 percent of revenues to about 30 percent of revenues.[4]

The broker now faces a situation in which the income derived from the pure brokerage of real estate is insufficient to

---

[3] That Re/Max represented a true revolution in real estate can be seen by tracking the decline in company dollar.

[4] Most large companies today use a system whereby agents pay a fixed amount for expenses and then, in effect, keep all commissions earned after that.

sustain a business. Smaller firms make up the gap through individual sales: The broker is also an agent and sells real estate for his or her own income. In larger firms (and smaller franchised companies) the gap is filled by ancillary revenue. Where allowed by law, the company likely also owns a mortgage company, a title insurance agency, an escrow business, etc. The commission income now paid to the agent is replaced by driving other transaction services through the brokerage's companies or separate companies in which the broker has ownership; this also creates ethical issues. *Profitability is now less a function of increasing numbers of transactions and more a function of capturing an increased share of each transaction.*[5]

For this strategy to be successful, the brokers must have access to the consumers. To sell the services that make up a transaction, they must be able to explain the value of the services and close deals with consumers directly. But, traditionally, the agents "own" the consumers. Agents recruit consumers, advise them, negotiate on their behalf, and generally retain contact. Traditionally, a broker had no information on a consumer until such time as the listing agreement or the contract for the purchase of a property was accepted. So, for a broker to have access to a customer in order to sell that customer a variety of ancillary services conflicted with the interests of the agent.

The Agent Business

The agent business had always centered about control of the consumer. Because most business came from referrals, new agents were taught to create a "sphere of influence" that generally consisted of family, neighbors, friends, and acquaintances who could be relied on to speak kindly of the agent and refer business when it appeared. Past clients and customers were continually reminded of the presence of the agent in the real estate business, so that when they again have the need for a real estate transaction, they will remember the prior relationship and call on the agent again.

---

[5] The exact nature of this process makes up the bulk of Chapter 6.

Agent compensation traditionally had been derived from commissions on transactions. So, the agent's income was dependent on building and retaining a large sphere of influence, because that meant participation in more transactions. Because the law required that an agent be associated with a broker in order to do business, that commission was split with the broker. As long as the industry adhered to a relatively homogeneous standard, the system worked: the agent owned the consumer and shared the commission with the broker.

Today, the conflict presented to the broker by the increasing share of the commission going to the agent and the need to develop ancillary income has its mirror image with the agent. The negotiation about the commission split is closely tied to the control of the consumer because the broker can increase the share of the commission going to the agent only if he can develop ancillary income by selling more of the transaction to the customer.

Complicating the relationship is the need for technology. The back-office systems that are now necessary to drive the transaction to a satisfactory conclusion for the consumer are expensive. It is very rare that an individual agent can afford all the tools now necessary to do business in the new economy.[6] For the most part, these tools will be provided by the broker-owner, usually in return for increased access to the consumer. The terms of this deal have yet to be fully worked out, but it appears to be a way to reunify the broker and agent businesses.

The Association Business

Given the structure of the REALTOR® organization, membership recruitment has never really been a concern. Licensees would join a member firm and in doing so, would then join the local, state and national organizations (as well as the MLS). The association, in return for the licensee's dues, provided networking and education opportunities, a Code of Ethics and dispute resolution process, public policy representation, and communication about industry developments and issues.

---

[6] It is interesting to note that the very top producing agents provide this infrastructure by using assistants and forming teams—in reality, companies within companies—to provide the specialization that increases transaction efficiency.

At its heart, an association is an information business, and like all information businesses, trade associations (including the REALTOR® organization) have been challenged by the new economy. This challenge operates on two different levels. At the member level, there are a variety of alternative sources for association services. Private education providers, often using distance-learning techniques, are competing with associations to provide necessary training for their members. As real estate firms consolidate, they find it increasingly efficient to hire their own public policy representatives to lobby for them on specific issues. And, of course, with the liberation of information through the Internet, the information function of the association became eroded.

On the association level, the spread of cheap technology and the democratization of information have introduced redundancies among the local state and national associations. It is now relatively cheap to perform at any one level the functions previously provided by all three. This has led to growing rivalries among the different associations. If you talk honestly with association executives in the REALTOR® organization, they will tell you that there is no real need for all three levels, because anyone can do the job of all three. (Of course, their level will be the survivor and is the essential one, with the others superfluous.)

All this has given rise to the concept of transactional membership. If the association delivers more value than it asks in dues, the members see a reason for belonging. Otherwise, they will walk. In the REALTOR® organization, this is a relatively recent threat, since the MLS, usually owned by the local association, has always been the magnet holding members in. With the spread of property information through the Internet, and with federal courts ruling that association membership is not mandatory for use of the MLS, REALTOR® associations are finding the need to become more relevant to their membership base.[7]

Associations have attempted to counter the erosion of their market position by extending their business lines. Generally, REALTOR® associations have attempted to provide a guide to

---

[7] The exception to this is the California Association of Realtors (CAR), which has lived with the disconnect between association membership and MLS membership for nearly two decades. It has thrived by developing a menu of services relevant to the businesses of its members.

technology and information for their members. They have introduced new products and educational offerings geared to bringing the members up to speed on the techniques necessary to thrive in the new economy. While these attempts have varied in their approach and in their success, they have brought the associations into competition with the other businesses in the real estate industry.

These attempts have brought associations into conflict with both their largest members and with the MLS. As they provide products and services designed to equalize knowledge in the business, the associations are working to neutralize the edge that size provides to their largest members. One of the benefits of size in the age of technology is the ability to offer a work environment that contains the best and most efficient tools. If the trade associations offer these to all members, large firms cannot leverage their advantage. More importantly, the trade association is using dues collected from the large firms' agents, leading them to perceive that they are paying twice for the same tools.

If the new offerings of the association are not being funded from dues, they are being funded from profit derived from the MLS. As we discuss below, MLSs are also under pressure to find a winning formula in the new economy. That formula, whatever it is, requires money. To the extent that the owner-associations require that an MLS deliver its surplus to them, it prevents the MLS from doing the thing it must do. In addition, associations will often require their MLSs to provide technology at a "least common denominator" level, in effect dragging along the least advanced of the associations' members at a time when the MLSs should be raising the bar on acceptable technology.

The MLS Business

The information revolution has affected the MLS as much as, perhaps more than, any other real estate industry business. The reason is obvious: MLSs are primarily in the information business, and technology has changed the terms of access to information. With the Internet providing an open platform for details about property for sale, the MLS is no longer the only game in town. In fact, given the quality of presentation on the

Net, it may not even be the best option for those seeking property information.

This has presented an identity dilemma for most MLSs. One response has been growth and the development of regional MLSs. Thus, the entire Washington, D.C.-Baltimore Metropolitan Standard Area (MSA) is covered by a single MLS, as are Philadelphia-Southern New Jersey, Denver, Seattle, and most of the Chicago area. This growth has allowed for the introduction of economies of scale as well as the ability to introduce new technology to allow members to accomplish transactions faster, cheaper, and better. While these developments have improved the viability of the MLS in the new economy, they do not leave the MLS without conflict with the other businesses of real estate.

In addition to the conflict of interest with the associations described above, the MLS has another issue with the REALTOR® organization. Through its relationship with Homestore, the REALTOR® organization has opened the door for the listing of property on the Internet.[8] While the bulk of these listings come from the MLS, Home Store has also provided brokers and agents with the opportunity to link their own Web sites to its site, and thus put their own listing directly on the Internet. This diminishes the perceived value of the MLS.

Despite the ability of brokers and agents to access the Internet directly, the core resource of the MLS is, after all, data. In the new economy, information has value only if it is transformed into knowledge. In the past, the MLS did this by organizing the broker's listings and allowing them to be searched by location, size, and particular features. With that function now automatic, with software accessible to virtually everyone, MLSs must find new ways to leverage the real estate data that reside on their servers. Modern marketing thrives on the use of information, and the data contained in its "mine" places the MLS in a potentially lucrative position with respect to market research.

Here is where the conflict arises. While it is generally agreed that the process of assembling information within the MLS adds value to that information and transforms it as a piece of intellectual property, there is some question about whether that

---

[8] As this book went to press, Homestore was involved in serious problems. However, Realtor.com has not been significantly affected.

transformation itself constitutes the creation of a new product. The brokers assert that they still "own" the listing. The MLS would like to be the owner of the information and therefore be able to leverage it in the marketing arena. This is a dispute with some very real stakes. The data-mining potential of the MLS represents a new business line that could ensure its success in the new economy. Real estate professionals have historically collected and discarded volumes of useful information. The MLS has the competency to capitalize on that information, if it has the license to use it in any way it can.

The four businesses of real estate (broker, agent, Association and MLS) have existed together for a long time. Until the revolution that created the new economy, however, their relationship was complementary and cooperative. Because the industry had an information monopoly and industry knowledge and experience constituted a significant barrier to entry, the functions served by each business could remain separate, and particular roles could be assigned without problem.

In the new economy, the lines between information businesses have blurred, and that has become true in the real estate industry. Now the relationship among the four businesses is competitive rather than cooperative. With each being able to execute more functions efficiently, the complementarity that had existed is no more. Each business is attempting to fashion new models to deal with the pressures and dictates of the new economy marketplace. That has brought them into direct competition, and requires that each find out what it can do so well that someone will pay them for it. We take up the specifics of these adjustments in Chapters 6 through 9.

THINKING ABOUT TECHNOLOGY

The entire business world has been altered by the impact of technology. The economy has gone through a revolution equivalent to that of the 1870s when we shifted from being an agricultural society to being a manufacturing economy. The wave that has engulfed American business has altered the distribution of power in the marketplace—from producers to consumers—and has generated a new mindset on the part of enterprises in all industries, including real estate.

Nothing will happen in the market unless consumers want it to happen. To be successful, producers need to understand and anticipate what consumers want and how they want it, and then be able to deliver it. Understanding and anticipating require an intensive investment in marketing. In fact, marketing has never been as important to businesses as it is now. Delivery means being not only the first to market but also the most efficient in production. All of this requires the use of information and production technology that will deliver product and services to the consumer faster, cheaper, and better.

Real estate practitioners must also face and overcome this challenge. But all the new technology in the market and the speed with which it changes can be confusing. Given the history and tradition of a business built on people skills, it's often difficult to think clearly about what to use and how to use it. Given the way in which real estate practice is evolving, i.e., toward an electronically enabled transaction, you can't afford to ignore the new tools. So, how do you think about technology? Following are some rules to ponder.

Three Stages of Technology

Every change in technology proceeds through stages. We can illustrate each of these by focusing on the automobile (and more specifically the internal combustion engine).

The Open-Mouth-Wonder Stage. The *first* stage is "Gee whiz, look at that!"—in other words, technology as a toy for the adventuresome. In the case of the automobile, for example, this occurred the first time folks saw a horseless carriage smoking its way down some rural lane. The livestock shied and ran away, but people gathered around it, inspected it, and marveled at this new contraption. For us, it was the "Pong" game in the airport lounge that fascinated travelers. In any technology, there are a few early adapters, people who get the machines first and use them to the amazement of their friends. For our current information technology, these were the folks who bought the Commodores and Ataris, using the 64K machines to balance their checkbooks and play rudimentary games.

They Make-My-Life-Easier Stage. The *second* stage of technology occurs when we use it to do the same things that we've always done, but differently. Again using the automobile, this stage saw the replacement of the horse with the motor on trucks and tractors and carriages. Instead of harvesting the crops using horses or oxen, we used a reaper powered by an internal combustion engine. The harvest was brought to market in a truck operating on gasoline power. We visited friends and family in an automobile. Eventually, the internal combustion engine so dominated our activities that we thought little or nothing of it, but our conceptions of time and distance were altered forever. All this happened because mass production lowered the price of these vehicles and made them accessible to the bulk of Americans.

This process should sound familiar, since because it mirrors what has happened with computer chips. As their price dropped and their power increased, they have become part of virtually everything we do, to the point where we are unaware of their role in making things happen. But we do know that we communicate faster and more accurately, produce things more quickly, and generally lead easier lives. We've changed the way we do the things we do. *We are right now firmly in the second stage of technology.*

I vacationed last year with friends on Cape Cod. It's a lovely place and I had a wonderful time. During the course of my week on the Cape, we were alerted to the fact that a friend of friends, a professional fisherman, had caught a huge tuna and would be on the dock at 7 that evening. Drinks in hand (after all, it was August and we were on vacation) we trooped down to the dock, where the fisherman's family and friends (numbering about 30) were on hand to give him a round of applause appropriate to his 650-pound tuna.

That last part was really nice. I began to think of what it would mean to any of us if, at the end of the day, our friends and colleagues gathered around and applauded our work efforts. I suspect we would all find it exhilarating. Then I began to wonder how all the folks got down to the dock at the right moment. (After all, fishing is a pretty solitary proposition.) As it turned out, the reason was pretty simple. Fishermen now carry cell phones. When the fish was caught, the fisherman was able to call and spread the word about his good fortune. In fact, he had even called a nearby boat that had a winch to help him get the monster out of the sea and into his own small boat. (The fish took up more than half the available deck space.)

So there you have it. A very old and very basic profession generated a very human moment by using some ordinary but still very modern technology. I take this as an analogue to the real estate profession. Right now real estate is in that second stage of technology; in fact, it's been there for quite a while. Several years ago, real estate professionals blew past the first stage of technology, when we crowded into bars to get our turn at that new sensation, "Pong." From there, we gradually and effortlessly assimilated desktops, fax machines, digital cameras, virtual tours, cell phones, laptops, and Palm Pilots into our tool kits.

Now, we use all these tools to do business in a different way—or at least we should. Cell phones and e-mail keep us in touch with our customers and clients at all times. Wireless modems and PDAs (like the Palm Pilot) allow instant access to all the data we need to cement a deal. Yet, like the tuna fisherman, we don't do different things; we just use better tools to do what we've always done better.

That's really the key. Consumers want faster, cheaper, better service. You need the tools to fulfill their wants, and those tools are electronic in nature. I can remember when handheld electronic calculators first hit the market. Every so often, there was a newspaper story or a TV item about a man with an abacus who solved math problems more quickly than one with a new calculator. Yes, he could compute faster. But he was using his tool to its fullest potential, while the other guy was just scratching the surface of possibility of the new technology.

As an experienced real estate professional, you can probably complete a transaction the old way faster that others can using the new tools. But it would be like the man with the abacus. To be ready to enter the third stage of technology, doing new things, you need to be able to use the new tools easily. Only then will you be able to use the transaction management platforms that will become the mainstream medium of real estate.

The real estate industry will enter this stage within the next three years, and when it does, meeting consumer expectations will require facility with new ways of communicating and treating information.

One thing that won't be lost, however, is the reception at the pier. Real estate has always been and will always be a very human process. Whether it's your colleagues at the weekly sales meetings applauding your success, the look on the face of new homeowners when they realize it's finally theirs, or the pride on the face of a seller when she shows you around the house that's been home to her family for several generations or for decades, the human touch will never leave the real estate business. But with the new tools, more people will be standing around your pier, cheering because of you.

The What's-Next? Stage. The *third* stage occurs when we use the technology to do new things. The automobile eventually changed the way in which we envisioned cities, enabling us to build out instead of up and to reduce density over ever wider space. Our earliest cities were seaports, because water transport was the major channel of commerce. The cities were compact and grew vertically, to enable the bulk of the population to access the port facilities easily.[9] With the automobile, motor transit became the primary channel and we could occupy more space. Hence cities grew out instead of up and suburbs were as important as the urban core. Contrast, for example, the geography of San Francisco, a city that developed before the automobile, with that of Los Angeles, a city that has no core because it was developed after the automobile.

In the current information technology revolution, we have not yet reached the third stage, so we can't tell what form it will take. But the future is tantalizing, and it's probable that you will spend a good part of the rest of your working life there. Always be aware of what stage of technology you inhabit. It will help you think more clearly about how to use tools most effectively.

---

[9] On this basis, there are only eight "real" cities in the United States: Boston, New York, Philadelphia, Baltimore, New Orleans, Chicago, San Francisco, and Seattle. This, of course, reveals my blatant East Coast and urban biases!

Things in This Life Change Slowly if They Ever Change at All

Bill Gates once remarked that we always expect innovation to happen more quickly that it does, but we underestimate its impact. The poster child for this observation is virtual reality. Virtual reality hit the public consciousness in the mid-1990s as the next stage of technology. It would revolutionize the way in which training occurred. It would allow for safe and accurate scientific experimentation. It would push our knowledge of the universe out beyond our expectations. In real estate, we could show houses without leaving the office. Now, at the beginning of the 21st century, virtual reality is still in the first stage of technology—a toy for the early adopters. In our new economy, the gap between innovation and widespread use is substantial.

There are some sound economic reasons for this. Most new technology is pioneered by start-up companies that operate on a shoestring and habitually seek financing to bring their products to market. The more publicity they can generate, the better their chances of receiving the resources they need to succeed. As it turns out, these new companies are often just research labs for the well-funded and market-positioned companies that can popularize and distribute the innovation. We're seeing this now in the failure and consolidation of start-ups in American business. All the new stuff will come back, but only after a while and under the brand of a well-known outfit.

The technology that will most affect your business will enter your life subtly and will have a major impact on how you do things. To understand this, think of the tools you used five and ten years ago versus the tools you use now. Then ponder how your life is different. John Wooden used to tell his UCLA basketball teams to "Be quick, but don't hurry." This is a good motto for you in considering which technologies will work for you. Monitor the market constantly, but don't hurry to grab at what seems to be the next good thing that comes along. The odds are that you have plenty of time to think before you jump.

Tools Can't Tell You What To Do, and Technology Is a Tool

Assuming that you are rational, you never pick up a hammer and ask the hammer what you should do. The hammer cannot tell you what the job is. Before you choose a tool, you need to understand what you are trying to accomplish. Picking up the hammer makes sense only if the result you're looking to accomplish will be helped by using a hammer. Before you use anything—even the telephone—you need to define the result that needs to be accomplished. Without that knowledge, it is impossible to choose the best technology.

So, the plan comes first. Before you can think about technology, you should have put together a strategic plan and a business plan. The strategic plan should focus on the long-term future and specify what you would like your business to look like in 10 or 15 years. The business plan should be short-term and specify the things you need to accomplish in the next 12 to 18 months to move you toward the long-term goal.[10] It is imperative that you take time to understand the future you wish to experience, the paths that will get you there, and the actions you must take to walk down those paths. Only then can you choose the proper tools to use on your journey. As the Cheshire Cat pointed out to Alice, If you don't know where you're going, any path will get you there. More aptly, as Yogi Berra is reported to have observed, "If you don't know where you're going, you may wind up somewhere else."

Know What It Does, Not What It Is

If understanding the end to be accomplished is one key to understanding technology, knowing what technology does is the other key. But all you really need to know is what it *does,* not what it *is.* I know nothing about electricity. I haven't thought seriously

---

[10] The elements of the strategic plan are found in Chapter 4, Jim Sherry and John Tuccillo, *Click and Close: e-nabling the Real Estate Transaction* (Chicago: Dearborn Financial Publishing Co., 1999). A sample business plan can be found in the appendix of this book.

about electricity since I took Physics as a high school junior. If you asked me to explain electricity, I might tell you that on top of Mt. Fuji, the ghost of Elvis is hurling lightning bolts into buildings all across the world. Somehow, I don't think that's the correct explanation. Here's what I do know: If I enter a dark room and I need light, at about waist height, and within a foot of the doorway there will be a toggle switch that, when pushed, will illuminate the room.

Taking your time to understand all the ins and outs of information technology is time taken away from thinking about your business, and that's a mistake. Let the technical types understand the processes. Similarly, you don't need to be a technologist to use tools. All you need to know is what the tool will do for you and for your customers. When you put together your business goals with knowledge of what technology does, then you can choose the proper tools for your practice.

The corollary here is that the best technology is the one that works for you. When I travel, I used to carry a lightweight laptop computer, my cell phone, and a paper calendar. This combination worked very well for me, until I got a PDA. I found that the ease of the electronic organizer made my life less messy. A different combination may work best for someone else. Your own technology need not be the very latest or even the very best. But it has to work for you.

Avoid the Extremes

The extremes here are the faddists and the technophobes. We all know the technophobes among us, the folks who view new tools as TECHNOLOGY, a dark and scary thing.[11] More common is a variation on this that takes the form of technology paralysis. The paralyzed know about Moore's Law (every 18 months the computing power of a chip doubles and its price

---

[11] The interesting thing here is the speed and ease with which real estate professionals absorb personal technology. From cell phones to wireless modems, each new invention has been adopted and used to make life a little easier. Yet, most REALTORS® are technophobes in the sense that they worry about the application of information technology to the real estate transaction.

halves) and know that as soon as they sign the credit card slip, their new technology-hardware or software—is obsolete. So they don't buy at all. They keep waiting and waiting and waiting. "Maybe someday voice recognition will be available...then I'll buy."

The faddist exhibits the flip side of this behavior. If it's new, they must have it—even if they don't know what to do with it. Just being the first in the office with the newest toy is a gratification they can't pass up. We've all seen the guy who walks into the office on Monday with the latest and greatest, only to let it lay on his desk gathering dust as he relies on the old technology.

Neither approach is fruitful. Paralysis generates inefficiency; no matter what the correct configuration of technology is, any job in today's world can be done better using technology. Everything you do can and will be done better with tools available today. But you don't need to be on the bleeding edge to establish your credentials as a techno-savvy professional. Success requires the right use of the right tools, so you need to know how to use what's available and choose what's right for your goals.

Little Things Mean a Lot, but Size Is Important

About 120 years ago, a farmer got tired of the bad state of rural roads. They were impassable quagmires in spring and fall and rutted obstacles in summer and winter. So he invented a simple device that could be dragged behind a team of horses and used to smooth and crown the roads. His device caught on with his friends and neighbors and greatly improved the roads, to the point where the post office could deliver mail directly to farms. In turn, this enabled Sears, Roebuck and Montgomery Ward to establish national mail order businesses that, one could argue, were the first ever American examples of e-commerce.

More recently, catalog sales have become more automated, with virtually all retailers having their own Web sites through which you can order goods. Even using the phone will put you in touch with a customer service representative who can access your file and its history. In either case, your order will arrive at your door a few days later in pretty much perfect condition. The reason why this is possible has only a little to do with computers and the Internet. Rather, the service you get is a function of bar codes on products. These increase the speed of putting the order together a hundredfold and allow the kinds of time frames catalog companies can offer for their services.

Often the most important changes are small and unnoticed. So don't be bedazzled by hype; look for the changes that will make you more successful. Weigh everything, large and small, by what it contributes to your business goals. Where size does matter, however, is in the pipeline through which information reaches you. When you build a house, you make sure that the size of the pipe carrying water into the house is sufficient to provide the pressure and volume you need. The bigger the pipe, the better the service. It's the same way with information. Pay attention to bandwidth and the opportunities that cable transmission and DSL lines offer in connecting you to the world at a faster rate.

One final thought. We are now in the second stage of technology, one in which we use it to do things differently. I had a pager when I was five years old, and so did my friends. It was our mothers calling us in for dinner. Electronics hasn't changed that aspect. The next stage of technology will be one in which we do different things. That's coming soon to the real estate business, and you will be called on to change the transaction process itself. Take the time now to understand how you can use technology to do things differently so you are better prepared to do different things later. And remember, the value you bring to the marketplace and to your customers is independent of the medium. Your ability to counsel, negotiate for, and make professional management decisions about the transactions of your customers is independent of the medium you use. Intelligent use of technology will make you much more successful, but only if you can build a value proposition that is compelling to the consumer.

Chapter 3

Why Do We Need
New Business Models?

Quite simply, a business model refers to the core architecture of a firm, specifically how it deploys all relevant resources (not just those within its corporate boundaries) to create differentiated value for customers. Historically, strategists were not particularly concerned with business models, because each industry had a standard model, and strategists assumed that model in that industry. [1]

We have looked at the degree to which the new economy has evolved and how it has affected the real estate business. The driving force in all this is, of course, technology. But beyond its direct effect in changing the way in which we do the things we've always done, technology has triggered a process that is fundamentally changing the entire real estate business. In this chapter, we look at specific changes that call into question the ability of the traditional real estate model to create success in the new economy. This, in turn, causes the need to look for new models through which to do business. The reasons for looking at new models are fourfold:

---

[1] Don Tapscott, "Rethinking Strategy in a Networked World," *Strategy and Business,* Third Quarter 2001, p. 38.

1. The consumer has become the driving force in the marketplace, and the standards of acceptable service have been raised.
2. Technology has revolutionized the manner in which information is aggregated, analyzed, managed, and transmitted.
3. The business is consolidating, and new players are entering the market.
4. Compensation systems are changing as the dynamics of the relationships among brokers, agents, associations, and MLSs are changing.

In this chapter, we look at each of these, relating them to the need to think through the value proposition you bring to the marketplace and the new ways to think about your business.

In each particular circumstance, these forces will be acting to a greater or lesser extent. Using this chapter in your business entails thinking through the degree to which each of these forces is present in your market and then looking at the models described in Chapters 6 through 9 to adapt the one that fits your business the best.

THE OLD MODEL AND ITS DEMISE

All real estate professionals grew up within the same basic model. Conventional wisdom held that the public would always come to the real estate agent or the real estate office when they wanted to transact real estate business. The reason for this was that the real estate professional was the central source for all the information in the marketplace about properties for sale and interested buyers. It was simply more efficient to use the real estate professional than to attempt to "do it yourself."[2]

Based on control of information, the old model emphasized the central role of the real estate professional as the controller of data. Consumers were forced to come to the real estate office if they were to accomplish efficiently their real estate goals. Customer service was molded to suit the aim of the real estate

---

[2] Of course, some do try it themselves; for-sale-by-owner (FSBO) sales average about 15 percent of all sales on an annual basis.

professional: to complete the transaction. Thus, the real estate professional was a gateway for the consumer. Before consumers could access all the pieces that were needed to successfully achieve their goal, they first had to visit the holder of the information. From there, consumers were placed in touch with financing sources, title insurers, inspectors, appraisers, attorneys, and just about anyone else who figured into the real estate transaction process. As long as real estate professionals controlled the information about the market, they had a ready-made market.

In this, the real estate business was no different from a lot of other businesses. The market created a place for companies who traded in information, as long as the information was not readily available to the general public. In some cases, like real estate and travel, the connection was clear and apparent. In others, it was a little more indirect. For example, the broadcast television networks enjoyed a monopoly on the eyes and ears of American households for many years. They leveraged this into a business model that traded airtime for dollars, whether from advertisers or entertainment producers.

Information technology has taken away the control previously enjoyed by each of these businesses. The Internet and the expansion of cable television, radio, and newspapers have created access to all information for all people.[3] Under these conditions, the market no longer pays businesses that merely convey information. Simply having information no longer constitutes an added value for consumers. The reduction in the number of travel companies, estimated to be 40 percent of the industry, is a testimony to how the market has changed.

For the real estate industry, the old model has been killed by the presence of real estate and financing information on the Internet. With the advent of Realtor.com, Home Advisor, and the myriad broker and agent sites, it is now possible for the aver-

---

[3] In addition, demographics have helped as well. A large number of late baby boomers, inspired by the Watergate investigative reporting phenomenon, have flooded the media with available labor. This, in turn, has boosted the supply of publicly available information through conventional sources. Following them, Generation X has tinkered with web technology to create sites for just about every purpose. Between the two groups, the supply of information is virtually endless.

The California Association of REALTORS® (CAR) Survey

Last year, CAR commissioned a survey of recent home-buyers, both those who used the Internet and those who did not. Some findings:

- Nearly a quarter of all Internet homebuyers found the type of house they wanted on the Internet.

- Most homebuyers (78 percent) found their REALTOR® on the Internet at a Web site that listed a home they were interested in.

- Most Internet homebuyers (97 percent) agree that "using the Internet helped them better understand the home-buying process."

- All Internet buyers agree that "using the Internet helped me understand home values better."

- 71% of Internet homebuyers were first shown the home they purchased by a REALTOR®

- Nearly all Internet homebuyers (96 percent) are very likely to use the Internet the next time they buy a home.

- The average Internet homebuyer visited 4.6 different Web sites (excluding mortgage sites) as part of the homebuying process.

- The average Internet homebuyer visited 2.6 different Web sites to get mortgage information.

- More than half of Internet homebuyers (54 percent) got their mortgages online.

- Internet homebuyers tend to have achieved a higher level of education than traditional homebuyers, are on average younger (37.3 years) than traditional homebuyers (42.9 years), and are somewhat more likely to be married (84 percent) than traditional homebuyers (78 percent).

- Internet homebuyers on average purchased more expensive homes than traditional homebuyers ($403,752 versus $321,950).

age consumer to obtain "starter" information on a variety of properties. While the consumer may still need to contact the real estate professional to get the address of the property, he or she will be better prepared and will have prescreened the market before that happens.

This will eventually place strong pressure on compensation paid for services rendered by the public for real estate services. Adding to this pressure is the availability of other real estate transaction services on the Internet. The public can now obtain financing information and can actually apply for mortgages on the Internet, as well as obtain other settlement services. This reduces the value of the gateway function previously served by the real estate professional.

The bottom line here is that information technology has increased the power of the consumer in the market. Consumers can now do more of the activities involved in the buying and selling of real estate for themselves before dealing with a real estate professional. To obtain consumers' business, then, real estate brokers and agents need to craft a value proposition that consumers find attractive. Doing so means understanding, anticipating, and meeting consumer needs in the real estate market. That means a new business model.

CUSTOMER SERVICE IS EVERYTHING, BUT WHAT IS CUSTOMER SERVICE?

The massive changes that have buffeted the real estate business (including the destruction of the old real estate business model) because of technological change are quickly cresting. The spectacular sales market of the past five years that has covered over so many of the mandates for change is now merely a memory. The market is becoming merely good, and that will intensify competition. With the passing of the boom market will come more consolidation that will be dramatic in its impact and significant in setting the pattern for the industry over the next 20 years.

As directly affected by technology as the real estate business has been, it has been the *indirect* impact of technology that has caused the most changes. The consumer has been the absolute beneficiary of technological progress and now enjoys much greater market leverage and shows far less brand loyalty. Sensing this shift, most businesses have tried to accommodate it by becoming more consumer-oriented.

I was flying to the West Coast and had upgraded, based on the seemingly endless supply of miles with which my business endows me. At the end of the journey, the flight attendant handed every passenger in the front cabin a card. It was the pilot's business card, and on the back was a personalized, handwritten note from the pilot thanking me for my business, hoping I had a great flight, and expressing the wish I would fly again with his airline.

It was a wonderful gesture, and a great piece of customer service. I freely admit that I was overwhelmed that the pilot would take time out to thank each of us in a very personal manner. He is clearly an individual who understands that the personal touch, even in such a noncontact (no pun intended) occupation as airline pilot, has a meaning in today's marketplace. And it meant so much more than simply appearing at the cockpit door after the plane lands to say a perfunctory goodbye.

Unfortunately, the airline was United. The summer of 2000 brought the hell of dealing with its accumulated labor and technical problems, which left a bitter taste in my mouth. I was canceled, postponed, and rerouted to the limits of my patience. The customer service gesture by this captain was simply not enough to erase those memories. I fly United more than any other airline, so I have some degree of equity built up. It is that equity, that sunk cost, that kept me with the company; a personal thank-you note would not have been enough to keep me coming back. I look to an airline to get me from one place to another on time and safely. Courtesy and friendliness are good things to get in the bargain, but they are sideshows to the main event.

Too often we believe that in the real estate business, the reverse is true. We believe that being good with people and sympathetic to their problems comes before meeting our customers' substantive needs. So the industry is populated with nice people who feel that people skills are all they need for success. That may have been true once, but it no longer is the case. Those skills are important, but no longer enough.

All through the economy, companies are using modern marketing and service techniques backed by technological infrastructure to deliver world-class customer service. From e-tailers to traditional bricks-and-mortar companies, in both the product and the service industries, your customers are being educated every day to what is possible in the marketplace. If you can't meet the standards others are setting for you, you will be seen as an inferior choice in the market. And no amount of empathy or friendliness will cover for that.

The modern consumer has two needs in the marketplace: to get products and services faster, cheaper, and better and to be treated as if he or she were the only customer. The best companies meet these needs.

In real estate, the first of these needs translates to reducing the time it takes to conclude a transaction and the stress that tends to build up as the transaction is evolving. There are now a variety of technological tools, either on the market or about to emerge, that will help you do that.[4] Within the next 24 months, the best real estate professionals will be using these to manage transactions in the same way they use electronic organizers to manage their time. Success requires that you apply the best tools possible to the service of the consumers with whom you deal.

Meeting the consumer's second need is also important and requires more than a smile and a telephone call. It requires that you really understand what drives each of your customers. It means using the information you collect on the households you deal with and using that to give each the impression that he is your only customer. Try this: After each transaction in which you participate, call the buyer and ask for an interview. At that meeting, review the entire process with the buyer and find out what you did right and what you did wrong. Determine what you need more of and what you need to eliminate. The information accumulated from these sessions will make you more understanding of, and more responsive to, the real motivations and needs of your customers.

In the play *Death of a Salesman,* the hero, Willy Loman, talks about a salesman's life as being out there with just a shoestring and a smile, and that when customers stop smiling back, it gets

---

[4] See Chapter 5 for more details on these.

scary. By understanding what consumers really value, you'll keep them smiling back.

THE INCREDIBLE SHRINKING INDUSTRY

Technology Creates Opportunities

One of the by-products of technological change is the shift it creates in relationships among industries. There is a classic story of how the Union Pacific Railroad defined itself as being in the railroad business rather than in the transportation business. Thus, when the Wright Brothers were experimenting on the Outer Banks of North Carolina, Union Pacific took no notice. Today, railroads are in decline and air freight has eclipsed rail. In fact, Federal Express took the concept one step further and pre-empted the U.S. Postal Service. And, of course, there is no Union Pacific Airlines.

The current changes in information technology have had a similar effect. They have blurred the lines between many different industries that trade in consumer finance information. Within real estate, this means that real estate companies, mortgage companies and title companies, all trade in the same marketplace and can, at least in theory, perform each other's functions. At the very least they can all compete for first access to the consumer.[5] In the broader marketplace, banks, securities brokers, American Express, and financial planners can all operate as full-service consumer asset management companies.[6]

---

[5] Several years ago, Countrywide Finance, one of the largest mortgage companies in the United States, ran a series of ads in which it suggested that before consumers look for houses they obtain mortgages. Getting to the consumer first gets you to the head of the payment line, generally a good place to be.

[6] The current fight between REALTORS® and bankers over bank participation in the real estate business is happening only because information technology has made business poaching a reality.

New Entrants

As this blurring of boundaries has occurred, new entrants have found their way into real estate. They range from new investors, such as Cendant and GMAC, to innovators such as Homestore and Microsoft. In addition, firms in other industries that are raising the level of service to the consumer are challenging the way that real estate professionals do their business. The new entrants all share one characteristic: They are all seeking to exploit synergies involving the real estate market that will increase their profitability. Beyond that, it is hard to make any generalizations.

Cendant is perhaps the most prominent firm to enter the real estate business from the outside. Basically a franchising business, Cendant seized on real estate as an extension of its holdings in the hospitality industry. It bought Century 21, ERA, and Coldwell Banker and has pursued a two-pronged strategy. On the supply side, it uses its size to provide tools to its franchisees at reduced cost, thus making them more efficient and more profitable. On the demand side, it uses advertising and marketing to attract consumers to its real estate brands.[7]

General Motors Acceptance Corporation (GMAC) comes into the real estate business with a different goal. Its overall corporate strategy is to be the one-source consumer financing store. It purchased the Better Homes and Gardens network in 1998. Hoping to leverage its connection with General Motors and the significant customer and employee base that brings, GMAC is trying to integrate real estate brokerage with its mortgage and consumer finance operations. Management changes on the real estate side have so far been a barrier to the achievement of this integration.

Mid-America Power was faced with the deregulation of power that would force it to compete in its traditional market area with other companies. In an effort to preempt the competition, Mid-America purchased seven real estate companies (the most

---

[7] In November 1995, shortly after he became president of the Century 21 franchise, Bob Pittman met with the senior staff of the National Association of REALTORS®. He explained this approach to the market by saying that even if Joe's Hamburgers has a 50 percent market share in a town, Joe stops sleeping at night when the first McDonald's opens. His intention was to position C-21 as *the* real estate brand.

prominent of which is Edina in Minnesota) throughout the Midwest. Its strategy was to be present at the point where consumers were most likely to make decisions about utilities, namely the real estate closing. Being there as the consumer made her decision would give it a large edge. The strategy was sound, but ultimately unnecessary. The real estate holdings were spun off in 2000 as Home Services, a publicly traded company.

St. Joe Paper is the largest private landowner in the Southeast. Through its Arvida subsidiary, it conducts extensive national and international development activities. The potential synergies with residential real estate brokerage are an obvious extension of these activities. In 1999, Arvida acquired Prudential Florida Realty in an attempt to realize these synergies. To date, the deal is working well, and Arvida remains a force in Florida real estate.

Each of these new entrants brings a new attitude to the business. Traditionally, the real estate industry has been run according to its own rules rather than those that govern the rest of American business.[8] The new entrants have come into the business because they saw the potential for the creation of profit by exploiting new opportunities or by integrating related functions. In either case, the bottom line has become far more important in real estate than it ever has been before. The commitment of new entrants to real estate is not an emotional one, as is the case with a great many current real estate professionals. It is a business commitment, and it will remain as long as the business is worth keeping.

Consolidation

The new emphasis on the bottom line has permeated all of the industry. By itself, it has made the business both different and more challenging. Added to this is the death of the information monopoly. This has forced everyone to find and create value for the consumer. The business is no longer automatic, and

---

[8] One major broker describes real estate as less an industry than a collection of tribes. Another has pictured real estate associations as congregations rather than trade groups.

it is no longer easy. Broker-owners now find that staying in business is a bigger challenge than any they have ever faced in the past. As a result, many of them are getting out and the business is consolidating faster than ever before.

I was talking recently with someone very knowledgeable about the California market and I asked him how many large (250+ associates) independent firms were left in the state. (The discussion was prompted by the sale of Fred Sands Realty to the National Realty Trust [NRT].) We thought about it for a while and came up with exactly three—in the entire state! The situation is much the same in virtually every state.

All around the country, real estate firms are disappearing either by being acquired by, or by affiliating with a franchise. Over the past 14 years, the number of independent firms has shrunk by about one third, from about 120,000 in 1987 to about 80,000 today. That shrinkage has largely been the result of the acquisition of smaller firms by larger independents and of large companies by external owners like the NRT.

This trend is accelerating, and in the future we will see fewer and fewer firms. The reason for the roll-up and the implications are both the same: Real estate is becoming an information-intensive business and the cost and reward of playing are both going up. The process is being driven by three factors, each of which is likely to continue in the near (five- to ten-year) future.

1. *Technology.* As we have seen, the impact of information technology development has been felt significantly in the real estate business. There is significant pressure now on firms to extend their use of electronic communication with both their associates and their customers in order to remain attractive to both. For sales associates, the business technology provided by the firm at a minimum must be as sophisticated as that available in their homes. At the maximum, it must equal the setup offered by the most innovative firm in the market. For consumers, the firm must be accessible to them in the way they find most comfortable and must provide them with all the information they feel necessary. This has raised the cost of doing business and cut into the profits of many real estate companies.

The economies of scale offered by size are attractive as an offset to this cost. The acquisition of hardware and software requires capital, and their maintenance entails an ongoing outlay. Yet, adding more agents to the system and using them to process more transactions add little to the total cost. Thus, the larger the size of the firm, the lower the per-transaction cost of technology and the greater the profit. There is thus a valid technological reason to grow larger.

On the other side of the coin, companies that cannot increase in size will find that the cost of keeping up with developments in the market is excessive. The cost of technology will cut severely into profits and reduce the competitiveness and viability of the firm. The sum total of both these effects is that bigger is better; thus, there is a tendency toward consolidation.

2. *Aging ownership.* There have been three great growth spurts for homeownership in the United States. The first occurred after World War II when returning GIs took advantage of the programs provided by a grateful government and settled the suburbs of most American cities. The second spurt occurred in the 1970s when the Baby Boom entered its first-time homebuying age. The third, and most recent, of these is still in progress and has coincided with the great technological change in the real estate business.

The great era of growth in the real estate industry coincided with these spurts in homeownership. Regardless of when they were founded, most major independent real estate companies grew dramatically during the first expansion of homeownership. Most franchises developed and expanded during the second surge.

As a result, most successful firms today are headed by owner-entrepreneurs who have built their firms from the ground up. They developed their companies as any small businessman develops a company, namely by paying attention to every detail and being involved in every decision. They have now reached an age where they are ready to retire. For the most part (again typical of most small businesses), they have not developed any second-level leadership. They could turn the business over to the kids, but is many cases the kids don't want to do it or there are no kids.[9]

This situation makes the owner very open to external exit strategies. This represents an excellent opportunity for an acquiring entity, whether an independent real estate company, a franchise, or an outside company. The acquirer comes in, buys out the owner at some multiple of income, and expands its operations. To save face, the acquisition can be dressed up as a merger, with the broker-owner keeping a nominal relationship with the new owner.[10]

3. *Aggressive buyers.* As we discussed above, the real estate business has attracted significant outside capital in the past several years. While this occurs periodically, this particular round is marked by the search for synergies that may not have been present in a less technological age. In the example mentioned earlier, Mid-America Power, faced with the specter of power deregulation, bought up a number of large Midwestern real estate firms and combined them into a public company, HomeServices. Other examples abound, but the bottom line is that money is aggressively seeking firms in the real estate industry.

In many ways, the real estate industry resembles the banking industry as it developed after 1980. In that year, the Congress passed a massive deregulation bill that removed the price and interest rate controls that protected banking. The result of those controls was a bloated industry that supported 18,000 separate

---

[9] Interestingly, this is less true for agents than for broker-owners. There are many cases where top-producing agents are joined in their businesses by children who become their partners and eventually take over the customer relationships.

[10] Sometimes the sale will occur even if the broker-owner is not looking for an exit strategy. In some cases, the offer is simply too good to refuse. In its early acquisitions, both Cendant and the NRT were almost legendary for overpaying. NRT would regularly pay five to six times EBITDA (a standard industry earnings measure) when firms were generally selling at about 60 percent of that. Cendant bought the ERA franchise system by outbidding its chief rival by a factor of two.

firms. By way of comparison, Canada, with a population one-tenth that of the United States, had a total of 14 banks at that same time. Deregulation brought market forces into play and the banking industry shrank. Now there are about 6,000 banking firms. Anyone who has seen his or her bank change names almost annually understands what has happened to the banking industry.

In real estate, the catalyst is not a piece of legislation but rather a technological revolution. The shift in technology has removed the barrier to information that formerly faced the public and protected the real estate industry. In its wake has come the inevitable consolidation of the industry. Will the real estate industry be reduced to a third of its size, as banking has been? The answer is probably not, because the barriers to entry into the real estate industry are far lower than those in banking. However, we have already seen a shrinkage of about one-third, with more on the way.

COMPENSATION SYSTEMS ARE CHANGING

There are two ways of grasping reality. You can look at it from outside and see how theory explains reality or you can experience reality and then try to fit some sort of order to it. Getting a complete picture often requires that both methods be employed. Too often, I find myself in the first position. So, periodically, I conduct informal surveys of real estate professionals whom I know to get a feel for what's really going on in the marketplace.

I did one recently to see what's changing in the business. Perhaps the most startling change to me is in the number of REALTORS® with whom I spoke who are adopting the fee-for-service approach to business. They will provide specific services to the customer and charge for each service, rather than providing an all-in-one package priced as a percentage of the house price. This is a reaction to consumer resistance to high commission dollars in an up-market environment, but it also reflects the fact that increasing numbers of consumers are techno-savvy and can do many pieces of the transaction by themselves.

Traditionally, real estate professionals offered a single price to consumers. All the services required for the sale of a house would be accomplished for a set fee, quoted as a percentage of the sale price. This worked well at a time when information was not generally accessible to the public. Now, as that has changed and consumers can do some pieces of the transaction for themselves, that pricing model is too inflexible to be acceptable in the market.

Over the past several years, we have seen the emergence of companies such as Zip Realty, eRealty, and Your Home Direct, with their different approaches to the business. By offering the consumer an Internet-based solution at a reduced price, they demonstrate to the industry the viability of alternative pricing models. By doing so, they have added to the movement. The single compensation model that most of the industry holds as gospel is ossified and inappropriate. There are pioneers on the frontier who are breaking new ground; the industry will follow. In Chapters 6 and 7, we look at new compensation models in greater detail.

A FINAL THOUGHT: TECHNOLOGY IS A MUDDLE

The first rule in thinking about technology is that things in this life change slowly, if they ever change at all. With the collapse of so many start-up companies over the past two years, the notion of a technological revolution and a new economy has been called into question. It seems now that little has changed: Firms come and go; we do the same things.

It's no different in real estate. Two years ago, we could see a bright new world of electronic transaction management: The many parts of the real estate transaction that could be automated would be automated; the role of the real estate professional would be diminished. Now, those promises have seemingly proven false. Companies that advertised the solution have gone out of business, and some of those who have not are trying to live up to promises made about systems still in development. Despite promises and predictions, there is no one system now available that will solve the riddle of the electronic transaction.

The result is a general disillusionment about the use of technology in real estate similar to that which has affected the rest of the economy. Trade shows, from the NAR's midyear meeting and its convention to Real Connect, are spiritless, and the feeling of inertia is palpable. Right now, there is no real winning system. Rather, there are tools. In fact, there are many tools, a number of which you will read about in later chapters.

The tone in the industry is beginning to switch from looking for a single answer to seeking the right tools that will enhance operations. Consistent with that, the search now has shifted from the single system to the platform that will allow firms and agents to "plug and play;" that is, to be able to link a wide variety of tools so that they work together. Think about your PC. You can build a system by hooking together components from different manufacturers because the standard to which they build is consistent. With real estate tools, the same process will be the answer.

All this doesn't mean the end of the knowledge revolution in real estate. Rather, it means that the hard work of building a business in a new environment is just beginning.

Chapter 4

The Critical Competencies

As the economy has changed, so have the rules of business. In an earlier book,[1] I outlined these new rules. But to execute successfully the rules in the new economy, a new set of competencies is required. Having these is a prerequisite to be able to survive and thrive. These competencies are

- counseling the consumer;
- negotiating the contract;
- managing the transaction;
- marketing;
- building and maintaining a brand;
- acquiring, managing, and using information;
- thinking strategically.

Understanding your core business competencies is crucial in a world where change is endemic and competition is coming from all sides. Following the same old path may help you reach retirement, but it isn't enough to truly succeed in the new economy. The consumer is getting faster, cheaper and better service

---

[1] See John Tuccillo, *The Eight New Rules of Real Estate,* Dearborn Financial Publishing, 1998.

from the raft of manufacturing and service businesses who "get it." You can't be an exception to that trend.

In this chapter we develop, explain, and implement these competencies. This is perhaps the most important chapter in this work. Regardless of the model you choose to follow, you must be able to master the seven competencies listed above if you are to be successful in the future. Also note that this chapter is not about technology. The tools you use have changed, will change, and probably will change rapidly. The value you bring to the market will not. The competencies you bring to the market will define the degree to which you provide value to the public.

WHAT BUSINESS ARE REAL ESTATE PROFESSIONALS REALLY IN?

Before all that, however, you need to be clear about your business.

Norm Brodsky writes a very interesting, enlightening and entertaining column in *Inc.* magazine. In one of his columns, he wrote about a friend who sold fish to restaurants and was extremely successful. Norm asked him for the secret of his success, and the friend explained that he was successful because he knew what business he was in. "Easy," replied Norm, "you're in the fish business." "No," said the friend, "I'm in the banking business." He advanced fish on credit to restaurant owners, who would later pay him for both the fish and the credit. Thus, his margin was derived not so much from the fish he sold but rather from the credit he advanced. Knowing that this was the source of his profit focused him much more clearly on the information, competencies, and tools he needed to run his business successfully.

American business abounds with examples of this seeming anomaly between the way the company seems to the public and the actual business it's in. McDonald's operates to maximize the value of the real estate it owns and the ground leases it controls. It does this by placing stores that will attract the public to that real estate and by controlling its product and delivery system with great intensity. Fast food is merely the channel by which McDonald's makes money from real estate. The company knows this and is very clear on how it implements its strategy. Similarly,

Nike is a marketing firm, Sara Lee promotes brands, and American Express specializes in secure documents.

Occasionally, a firm can get into another business quite by accident and then adjust its strategic approach to profit from the change. One of the highest profile examples of this is the Chrysler Corporation. In the late 1970s, the federal government bailed out Chrysler, which was near bankruptcy. Shortly thereafter, interest rates and inflation skyrocketed as the economy sagged. Vehicle sales were down, but Chrysler was making a great deal of money on its financing arm. In fact, the revival of Chrysler was attributable to its role as a banker, rather than as a vehicle manufacturer. Subsequently, Chrysler embarked on an expansion and acquisition program that leveraged its competency in consumer finance.

It's extremely important to know what business you're in, so that your strategies and actions are effective in the marketplace. For real estate, the normal focus is on land and buildings, i.e., the product that is marketed. Real estate practitioners don't buy or sell land and buildings. Their role as agent rather than principal ensures that.

Real estate professionals have always served as a main conduit of information in the marketplace. And as technology has changed the manner in which we deal with information, their business has again shifted. Now, information is not enough. Consumers can get that on their own. Rather, real estate professionals must serve as knowledge brokers between those who wish to transact real estate. Information must be made actionable so that consumers can get what they need when they need it in an acceptable manner. The real estate professional must know enough about the market and about the consumer to be able to anticipate the needs of the consumer and satisfy those needs better than anyone else.

So, the business of the real estate professional is the maintenance of a consistently excellent channel of knowledge to consumers involved in the transaction of real estate. All this means that any successful business model must take into account both the desires of the consumers involved and the changes that have taken place in information technology.

Yet, knowing your business is not enough. To execute, you need to possess certain core competencies that allow you to implement the plan you devise. A classic case familiar to most real

estate professionals is NAR's misadventure with the REALTORS®
Information Network (RIN). The concept was good: It was a strategic attempt to address the changing information technology that
has affected the real estate business. The problem was in the execution. To create a successful technology subsidiary, NAR needed
a competency it did not possess. Yet, it made the decision to create
and operate the subsidiary in house, thus dooming it to failure.

As you read the next sections, keep in mind that a good plan
remains a fantasy if the proper competencies and tools do not ac-
company it. Also keep in mind the fact that competencies, like
tools, need not be home grown. It is possible to acquire a competency through strategic alliance, through joint venture, or
simply by buying it.

COUNSELING THE CONSUMER

If you look at the real estate transaction as it has been affected by information technology, it is apparent how much
control consumers now have, and how much more they will have
in the future. Web sites, from Realtor.com to Home Advisor to
the most local brokerage site, allow consumers to search for
homes and prescreen houses of interest. The home financing
process has been placed online as well, so that consumers can
enter the search process already qualified for a mortgage. E-mail
and calendaring tools allow for the scheduling of appointments
for the closing process.

In the near future, title searches will be available online so
that the vast majority of properties will come onto the market
with clear title. Appraisals, to the extent they exist,[2] will eventually move to the Web, and houses will come onto the market with
a lender-approved appraisal attached. Software already exists
that allows for the simultaneous handling of documents in several locations, and Congress has approved electronic signature
recognition for legal transactions.

---

[2] Lenders, including Fannie Mae, are already moving away from the worth of
the property as a key factor in the loan process. Rather, they are relying far more
heavily—almost exclusively—on the credit of the borrower and are using appraisals
simply to check on the existence of the property. In the near future, traditional appraisals will cease to be part of the homebuying and selling process.

When this comes together, the time from home search to closing will take a few days rather than the one to three months it now takes. This is not to imply that all buyers and sellers will be able to move within a few days. Indeed, the moving process will still take longer. But the time-abbreviated real estate transaction will allow the timing of the move to be at the discretion of the consumer, not (as it is now) at the hands of some other entity in the real estate process—mortgage company, real estate professional, attorney, title insurer, or other. This is consistent with the general shift in market leverage toward the consumer that has been the hallmark of the information revolution.

As the technology allows the consumer to control the transaction, the traditional role of the real estate professional will diminish. There is no longer a need for, nor will the market reward, the transmission of information by hand. Showing of houses will increasingly be an automated function.[3] Relationships with mortgage lenders will carry less and less importance. And, of course, the paper management function will go away.

So what's left? Will the REALTOR® disappear? The answers: Plenty and No.

Perhaps the most important informational effect of the Internet has been the availability of medical information. From access to medical dictionaries and case studies to the existence of user groups devoted to different illnesses, laymen now have an unprecedented volume of medical information at their disposal.

Recently, I was "asked" by my doctor to undergo some diagnostic testing. While the probability was that nothing serious was wrong, there was some chance that the results could cause me to radically change my view of the future. Before I had the tests, however, I went online and searched everywhere I could for information about the test, its after effects, the potential for serious illness, and the various treatment options now available. I was able to gather a huge amount of information, so that the tests lost their mystique and I was fully prepared for any result.

---

[3] Once again, this will be to the benefit of the consumer. The recent technology survey by the California Association of REALTORS® (December 2000) indicated that consumers who used the Internet as part of the homebuying process physically saw only one-fifth the number of houses as did those who did not go online, and they were able to find their homes in one-fourth the time.

Fortunately, the test revealed no medical problems and I went on my merry way. I did my research and learned a great deal about what might be happening to me. Yet, I would not have to forgo the use of a physician. Even if I could have performed the test by myself and seen the results firsthand, I still needed the experience and expertise of the doctor to tell me all the ramifications of my condition. In other words, the physician was more a counselor and analyst to me and less an information provider.

Sound familiar? Well, it should. The impact of the Internet on medicine is close to the impact on real estate. Think about it. Consumers can go to the Internet, find homes for sale, and see visual representations of the homes. They can then go to neighborhood Web sites and find details about living in a particular area, complete with maps. Yet, to truly understand the full dimensions of house and neighborhood, consumers must still rely on the specialist, the real estate professional who can tell them about things that don't appear on the Internet.

In other words, real estate professionals bring context to home buying and selling decisions. This is a departure from the traditional role of the real estate professional, but not a large one. They have always served as counselors to the consumer, but this was subordinated to the function of providing information about properties available and exposing properties for sale to the entire market. That old function gave the real estate industry a central place in the transaction, and thus a right to compensation. That right has become clouded because of the emergence of the Internet and the empowerment of the consumer.

Becoming a counselor to the consumer is less a reinvention of the REALTOR® than it is a mental redefinition. The real estate agent and broker are still intermediaries in the transaction process. But now the nature of that intermediation must be changed. The information function must be deemphasized, while the counseling function must be elevated.[4] This is a shift in

---

[4] In *The Eight New Rules of Real Estate,* I described how mass-market booksellers have adjusted to the emergence of Amazon.com. One, Borders, has shifted the middle to emphasize its function as an adult gathering place. The movement toward counseling and away from information provision is the same shift.

self-definition. You have to be clear to yourself about how you bring this competency to the market.

Make no mistake; the consumer expects counseling as a major service feature from the real estate professional. You need to exercise this core competency if you wish to be successful in the new economy. Fortunately, it's relatively easy to present this value proposition to the market, because it's already part of your tool kit. Realtors have always been counselors.

The way to work this into your market is to change the way in which you promote yourself. The public increasingly doesn't care about how many millions of dollars worth of real estate you sold last year, how many listings you have, or what designation initials follow your name. Rather, the consumer is interested in how you can help him or her find the perfect house for the best price in the shortest period of time. In other words, while REALTORS® promote themselves through the use of *features* (sales, listings, education, etc.), the public expects to hear about *benefits.*

Your listing presentations should be lighter on credentials and heavier on case histories. How many individuals in similar circumstances to the target household have you helped and how have you helped them? How much do you really know about the needs of this particular consumer and how will you fill those needs? Unless you can present yourself as the counselor who can provide singular benefit to a consumer, you are in the position of asking for a fee to do what consumers can easily do for themselves.

NEGOTIATING THE CONTRACT

With all the technological improvements that have been made in the real estate transaction and all that are yet to be made, there are certain essential human moments that will never pass away. One of these is the point of contract, when an agreement on the terms of a sale is reached. In normal markets, when there is neither an abundance nor a dearth of supply, this point is dominated by skilled negotiators.

Most people hate confrontation; they will go out of their way to avoid dealing directly with a situation that requires disagreement with others. As a result, they're no good at it. Negotiation is a form of confrontation and, as such, represents a market skill that consumers will buy. Real estate professionals are expert negotiators.

Too often this competency has been underemphasized in real estate promotion. It is clearly important and valuable to the consuming public and will command value in the market. It needs to be a central message in your approach to the public. Interestingly, the promotional ads being run periodically by the National Association of REALTORS® features this competency. The tag line of the ads is "You have a life; we let you live it. We're REALTORS® and real estate is our life." One of the specific spots talks about a teacher who is meeting with parents while her REALTOR® presents a contract on a house she wants to buy.

This time the NAR got it right. Negotiating on behalf of the consumer is one of the major value-adding activities that the real estate professional can perform. It ought to be featured front and center in any representation you make to the public.

MANAGING THE TRANSACTION

Ask a real estate professional about the two biggest costs of the real estate transaction, and they will mention the real estate commission and the financing costs. Ask a consumer and they will tell you that the major costs are time and stress. From contract to close, a real estate transaction currently takes four to six weeks (although, as we discuss above, that time will be reduced drastically in the future). During that time, there is always a degree of uncertainty as to whether the deal will actually go through. Both these factors weigh heavily on the consuming public.

Adding value to the principal in the real estate transaction will involve reducing the time it takes for a transaction to become a reality and ensuring that all snags in that process are cleared up seamlessly. That means managing the transaction. Providing the buyer and seller with an efficiently managed transaction is one of the most valuable services that real estate professionals can provide.

There are a number of ways in which this can be done. Traditionally, the REALTOR® uses brute labor to make sure all is in order. The real estate transaction process involves telephone (and now e-mail) contact, the physical transportation of documents, and face-to-face meetings with vendors. Parts of this process can be automated using off-the-shelf software like Microsoft Outlook and Top Producer. But for the most part, it is a time- and labor-intensive process.

This tradition is the major reason why surveys indicate that real estate professionals spent a great number of hours each week at work. It is also cumbersome, and it reduces real estate professionals' earning capacity by tying them up with chores that could more easily be done by less qualified individuals.

The most prolific producers have refined this process somewhat by building teams of assistants whose function is to execute some portion of this paper chase. This allows specialization and conserves the REALTOR®'s time for listing, counseling, and the other customer relationships at which the professional excels. This is a better way for two reasons. First, it increases efficiency by dividing the work. Specialists can work more quickly and more expertly if they repeat the same functions again and again. Second, it allows for more personal relationships with principals, who are touched by the real estate *team* more frequently than they ever could be by an *individual* real estate professional. Of course, this approach only makes sense when volume allows. Thus, it is most often used by top producers.

Another way of managing the transaction is by using electronic systems, many of which are currently in development. All exhibit the second stage of technology, in that they are tools for doing the same things differently. First, all communication necessary to the transaction is automated through either e-mail or intranet connection. This allows for all participants in the transaction to be apprised of progress instantly and simultaneously. Second, parts of the system allow the real estate professional to organize contacts and listings. The ability to link prospect and customer names with property descriptions allows the agent to provide instantaneous customized service.

The essence of these electronic transaction management systems is in the process that takes the transaction from contract to closing. Here virtually everything is automated. Essential services like title, appraisal, escrow, and closing are arranged via e-mail in which the relevant parts of the contract are transmitted to the appropriate service vendors. Tracking systems flag parts of the transaction that are lagging behind schedule and allow the real estate professional to attack problems as they appear.

Most of the systems being developed will include electronic forms so that information from the contract can be distributed throughout the system and the forms developed electronically. Eventually, these systems will include asynchronous handling of documents and electronic signature recognition. These will further squeeze down the time needed for the transaction.

These electronic systems are not yet ready for market.[5] But their importance is undeniable. As we shall see in Chapter 5, they are serving as the centerpiece of new business models being employed by real estate firms. In the very near future, they will set the standard for industry practice. The consumer will expect the service they provide, and they will be basic tools for any credible real estate professional.

Before that point, there are improvements that still can be made in the traditional transaction management process. The industry standard may seem to be personalized service carried out in a labor-intensive manner. The reality is that the most successful practitioners have already raised the standard. They have created the human equivalent of the electronic transaction management systems that are in the future. You no longer can do it alone, all by yourself, and hope to delight your customers. You need to develop a system that leverages your time and individual talents. In some cases, that can be done by intensively using prepackaged software to accomplish some tasks. In other cases, it can mean relying on an assistant. But it clearly isn't driving around town with a pile of papers in the back seat. That's not in the job description.

---

[5] There may not be any complete systems out there, but there is a lot of "vaporware." Many firms have claimed the invention of a transactions management system, but there is nothing out there that can be called *complete*. Some of the companies have folded (see Chapter 1), and others have introduced partial systems. Perhaps the highest profile of all of these is the e-Realtor platform of Homestore; unfortunately, it is some time away from completion, and, given Homestore's financial problems, may never be completed.

MARKETING

As information becomes free, knowledge gains in value. Knowing what is available is less important than knowing if what's available meets your needs. From the viewpoint of the real estate professional, this translates into an emphasis on marketing. In the past, marketing in the real estate industry consisted of advertising. The decision process consisted of what the ad would look like, where it would go, and how often it would run. A yard sign and several open houses completed the marketing plan. With the exception of high-end homes or unique properties, this was pretty much the sum and substance of marketing.

The spread of information has increased consumer expectation of what will be done to market properties. To begin with, their choice of media has shifted. The recent California Association of REALTORS® survey indicated that 89 percent of buyers who use the Internet started their process of home search before consulting an agent. This suggests that a strong Internet presence is key to marketing a property successfully.

It goes beyond that. Consumers have been educated by a variety of other industries (most notably hospitality) to want to be catered to and cajoled. They have come to expect that marketing will be customized and personal. And they want to see benefits. Real estate has relied on somewhat impersonal methods of marketing that stress features. Consider the standard farming process. The agent blankets a neighborhood with postcards announcing that he has listed and sold a certain house and this year will have sold $x million worth of properties. Contrast that with the approach of Amazon.com, which analyzes the buying habits of the individual and then creates personalized lists of products to offer to the consumer. In the first case, I'm receiving information that has little effect on me (unless I feel good that houses in my neighborhood are rising in price). In the second, I'm getting information that is actionable, i.e., knowledge.

The successful real estate professional in the new economy must have competency in marketing. This means modern marketing techniques. In traditional marketing for other industries, marketing has consisted of the "four *P*s": promotion, product, place, and price. REALTORS® have expertise in creating the product for market and pricing it. One might argue that the product is out of the hands of the real estate agent. This is only partially true. The basic physical structure and its location are given and fixed. But its presentation to the market is not. The real estate professional with any experience knows what appeals to potential buyers and is able to shape the "product" through cosmetic changes.

The pricing of the product is, of course, central to real estate success. It is also often the most difficult. REALTORS® have sufficient understanding of the market and access to enough information about recent sales to recommend the correct price. But in any market, it is a truism that sellers are always the last to know. They trail the market, overestimating the value of their property as the market slumps and underestimating when the market recovers.[6] Often the judgment of the REALTOR® and that of the seller fail to coincide, making the pricing process a negotiation (see the second competency at the beginning of this chapter).

It is in the areas of promotion and place that the marketing competency may be weak. Marketing concepts come and go like fashions. Now, however, the prevalence of information has been recognized as a key to successful promotion. Amazon.com, among others, tracks and logs consumer behavior until a profile of buying habits emerges. That profile will then be used to market specific books and music to specific consumers. My profile is different from yours, but both of ours fit us perfectly.

As another example, manufacturers of kitchen appliances monitor use by consumers through direct observation. Cameras are placed in kitchens (with permission, of course) to tape how consumers use their products. This allows manufacturers to understand not only what appliances consumers use and how they use them but how they use them together. That information feeds into the promotion of both individual products and groups

---

[6] Occasionally, real estate professionals will take advantage of this. A widow in my neighborhood was preparing to sell her house and move to an assisted-care facility. She interviewed four agents, three of whom suggested roughly the same price. The fourth suggested a price $50,000 higher. Flattered, the seller listed with the last agent. The house remained on the market for eight months and finally sold for the price agreed on by the first three agents. The price the woman paid was far more than the $50,000 she "lost."

of products. In essence, they are not selling a physical object but the answer to an unarticulated but real need.

There are two elements to this story. The first element has to do with the accumulation and use of information: The appliance manufacturers developed information on consumer habits and then applied that to their marketing efforts. The second element deals with marketing as the process of understanding what consumers want and then tailoring products to those needs. Both of these have relevance for real estate marketing.

The data element of marketing is one in which real estate professionals have not exhibited proficiency. They regularly solicit personal and financial information from customers and clients that could prove as useful in marketing efforts as the hidden cameras of the appliance manufacturers. In other industries, this information could be used to create pictures of consumers that would allow the personalization of marketing. But despite possessing in their files all the information they need to create consumer social and financial profiles, real estate agents destroy this information.

Ideally, the real estate professional would, in a listing presentation, indicate the specific geographic areas in which she will position the information about the property, based on an analysis of both the property characteristics and consumer homebuying habits. Yet, this is rarely done. We discuss later in this chapter the competency of amassing, analyzing, and using data, but the marketing competency goes beyond that. It entails a mindset that is not currently at work in the real estate industry to any great extent.

Developing this marketing competency is harder than acquiring it. This is a case where specialized help should be sought, either through hiring someone to exercise this competency or through a strategic alliance with a marketing firm in your area. Before you do that, however, take some time to read the current business press. In particular, pick up *Business 2.0, Fast Company,* or *Red Herring,* all magazines that have interesting and readable articles on the state of modern marketing.

One last word. Recently, a Gallup survey[7] suggested that there is a fifth "P" in marketing. In a study of fast-food operations, the survey discovered that people are the most important factor in determining repeat business. This appears to be more applicable in service industries, like real estate. And it's good news for real estate, since it has always been a people business. But that is an asset only if you have some quality control over the people who represent you. In other words, your people have to help you build a brand.

BUILDING AND MAINTAINING A BRAND

No one ever walked up to a McDonald's restaurant and wondered whether this one would be any different from the others. That's just not going to happen in this world. The key to McDonald's success is to repeat the formula time after time after time. You can close your eyes and describe the sights, sounds, smells, and noises of each and every McDonald's in the United States. It has to be that way: Branding requires that you do it the same way every time. And McDonald's pays fanatical devotion to maintaining consistency. Their training program is systematic and complete. They control their supply chains. All their buildings are the same.[8]

It's like that with every successful brand you can think of. Each is consistent with respect to colors, products, prices, and processes. You will never get fast service at Starbuck's but you'll enjoy the smells, the sights, and the music (all the same, everywhere). Being like this is important because it creates automatic responses from consumers that transcend the decision function. In other words, you don't want the customer thinking about where he is until he's already there. Increasingly, in times of change, consumers look to brands for assurance and consistency.

Branding is not a characteristic of real estate. While there are nameplates in the industry (Coldwell Banker, Re/Max, Long and Foster, etc.), there really are no brands as other industries have them. The experience received by a customer dealing with a real estate firm varies with the place and time the consumer encoun-

---

[7] *Gallup Marketing Journal,* May 2001, p.5.

[8] When the Roy Rogers franchise went out of business, McDonald's acquired one of its locations in my neighborhood. Now, fast-food restaurants are pretty much all the same, so with some minor refitting the store could have been reopened as a McDonald's. Not so. McDonald's razed the building and then constructed its own store on the spot.

ters the firm and with whom he meets. The face of the firm is that of its best and of its worst agents. The look of the firm differs from office to office, because the offices are created as opportunity permits rather than according to some sort of plan.

The capacity to build and maintain a brand is important to success in the new economy. It allows consumers to absorb and recall a great volume of information at the sight of your logo, thus saving them decision time and the effort of choice. It also allows you to focus on the value proposition you are offering the consumer in the marketplace rather than expending effort trying to establish an identity from scratch in their minds.

Building and maintaining a brand is a simple but arduous process. It requires two major resources: funding and determination. The funding is necessary because consumer opinions form slowly and require constant prodding to remain firm and fresh. That said, this competency is not solely reserved for large organizations. Branding can be done on the enterprise level, but individuals can do it as well.

The second resource, determination, is more important than the first. This is especially true in real estate, where the independent contractor relationship holds. The enterprise has only limited control over what it can force its contractors to do. But branding requires just such consistency and control. All members of the firm have to exhibit the same look and the same approach to the public, and each must submit to the control of the "brand police," those in the company charged with responsibility to ensure that the brand holds in the marketplace.

One of the biggest aspects of branding is how the offices of the company look and operate. Like a McDonald's, every company store ought to be set up exactly the same, so that any consumer entering will know exactly where everything is located. That means building offices rather than refitting available buildings. It's more expensive to do it that way; that's one of the reasons why building and maintaining a brand requires funding.

In those offices, the process to which consumers are subject is identical office to office. This includes how they are greeted, what information is provided, and all the steps they go through to complete a transaction. The colors, sounds, and feel of the office should all be consistent as well.

How do you go about branding yourself or your company? Once again, some outside help is probably necessary. There are companies and individuals that specialize in branding, and they can be a resource to give you the competency you need. Internally, though, you need to reorganize your operations in such a way that the creation of a brand becomes a priority. That requires physical changes, but also a cultural change. This is especially true for real estate companies that must deal with independent contractors and convince them that company branding will benefit them as well.

ACQUIRING, MANAGING, AND USING INFORMATION

Real estate is increasingly competitive, especially as the new economy increases the number of competitors. The ability to reach the consumer early in the process, to be the first point of contact, is an increasingly valuable competency. Doing so will require that you know how to acquire, manage, and use information. Let's examine the process of contacting and marketing the property of potential clients who live outside your market area. Without information competency, these potential clients are outside your reach. Yet, you could sort through absentee owner property databases and select pictures of available properties. You load these data into your computer, match the name and address of the owners, and get their e-mail addresses from a directory. You send the information package to the current owners, including investor financing, current value and equity, and a portfolio of your competencies and credentials. This approach has a high probability of getting you a new client, and that probability increases the more the new economy takes hold.

The average REALTOR® collects a mountain of data, information that professional marketing firms would pay a ransom for. Every transaction yields information about buyers, sellers, properties, and the details of the transaction itself. Combining these data with data-mining software, modern communications tools, and Web access creates the opportunity both to serve the consumer more efficiently and to increase the revenue derived from each transaction.

Capturing and using the information to which you have access is key to building a successful business in the new economy. Managing these data is critical to development of a value-added function in your business. Doing this requires the creation of a data management plan that:

- recognizes which elements of available data are of use now and in the future,
- integrates information from all areas of your operations,
- identifies the software and hardware that will run the system,
- keeps the information updates,
- provides for expansion and overhaul of the system capacity, and
- allows for new data and new uses.

Most importantly, as in the case with branding, the data management plan must be available to all employees, its importance stressed and its structure adhered to.

There are three major concerns for real estate professionals in developing a competency in acquiring, managing, and using information. The first of these deals with ownership of the data. The conventional wisdom in the real estate industry is that the information about the customer belongs to the agent while the information about the property belongs to the broker. Thus, any information management system hinges on the cooperation between the two. (There's that negotiation thing again!) As these two businesses of real estate diverge (See Chapter 2), this cooperation becomes increasingly difficult. This is especially true if there is to be revenue derived from the data management process. But, that prospect could be the carrot that brings both to the table to hammer out a common system.

The second issue deals with technical expertise. As we will see in Chapter 6, large firms have hired the technical facility they need to execute a solid data management plan. For smaller firms and individuals, the task may well be harder. Doing so will require resources and cooperation. The resources are needed to buy the expertise that is required. The cooperation will come, in all likelihood, from academics who are willing to consult with real estate professionals about creating systems to acquire, manage, and use information.

There is an overiding third concern: privacy. Consumers believe they own both their data and the data about their property. Government regulation in this area will grow.

STRATEGIC THINKING

In the new economy, change is the absolute. Because of that change, creating a strategic plan and then attempting to adhere to that plan is a pipe dream. In somewhat confusing terms, it can be expressed as follows:

> If you plan strategically for the future, what happens will surprise you, and you will be surprised that you're surprised. But if you think strategically about the future, you'll still be surprised by what happens, but you won't be surprised that you're surprised.

So, what's the difference between strategic planning and strategic thinking? It boils down to the starting point for strategy. In a plan, you begin with today and move toward the future. In strategic thinking, you begin with the future and work back toward the present.

Developing the competency to think strategically requires discipline and focus. To think strategically, you must first create a vision of the future.[9] This entails choosing where you want your business to be in 10 to 15 years. In essence, this is what you want to be when you grow up. It has to be a reach, something that is not easy to attain, but if it is attained, would create a world that you wish for greatly. To make this envisioned future real to you, you ought to describe how this state of reality looks, feels, tastes, smells; in other words, it should be as vivid as possible, to keep you moving toward it.

---

[9] The model for strategic thinking described here is derived from a model outlined in James C. Collins and Jerry I. Porras, "Building Your Company's Vision," *Harvard Business Review,* September-October 1996, pp. 65-77.

Having specified the long-term goal, everything you do should be geared to move you toward that end. Every decision you make should be made with progress toward the ultimate end as the criterion. You begin by identifying the major obstacles that lie between you and the envisioned future. Your plan should address those obstacles in general terms to give you an outline of the direction in which you need to move your business, the resources you will need, and the people you must have with you as you pursue your goal.

From that point, you move your thinking a little closer to the present. The question to ask yourself is What has to happen if I am to move to where I need to be in the next five years? What about the next two years? Finally, you can create a business plan for the next 12 to 18 months. This is what you can rely on for the immediate future.

Strategic thinking requires that you be prepared to switch directions in the short term with the caveat that you must adhere to your envisioned future. You can thus adjust to changing conditions (and you know they will change) easily without compromising the integrity of your business.

These are the seven most important things that you can do to prepare yourself for doing business in the new economy. If you do nothing else with your business, develop and/or acquire these competencies for your operations.

Chapter 5

Tools for the
New Economy

In Chapter 2, we discussed how to think about technology. One of the observations made was that any set of tools would work as long as they allowed you to reach the end you sought. That's true, but with a major caveat. Regardless of your goals, using pen, paper, and telephone ain't gonna get you there. There are folks out there in the real estate industry who are pushing ahead with technology that is letting them do a whole variety of things with ever-increasing speed. On the other side of the table, consumers are being constantly educated as to the possibilities open to them and are expecting to deal with businesses that use modern tools.

So you need some basic set of technology tools to enable your business to become a viable choice in the marketplace. Choosing these, however, can be a very difficult process. The numbers of machines, software programs, and vendors in the market is dizzying. Unfortunately, the most easily "acquired" product in the new economy is vaporware. Claims and counterclaims, unverified by the vendor and unverifiable by the consumer (owing to lack of technical knowledge), cloud the decision process.

Alas, this chapter is not the panacea you seek. Quite frankly, if I had the perfect answer, I could make far more money selling it in the market instead of practically giving it away in a book. Rather, in this chapter we try to do three things:

1. Describe the way to think about the basic setup that any real estate professional needs to be minimally qualified in the new economy.
2. Discuss enhancements to that setup and how these can be used.
3. Indicate where and how training can best be acquired.

We look at a basic tool kit because the new economy is, in some ways, dictating to you how you must do business. The essential rule is this: You must be as technologically sophisticated as your most sophisticated customers and be accessible and attractive to your least sophisticated customers.[1] The definition of "basic" will reflect the customer base that You serve. For some, it will be a higher bar than for others; for all it will be an ever-rising bar. At this end of the chapter, we present a list of the components of one successful agent's tool kit.

At the end of this chapter, you should be more knowledgeable about what the new economy requires of you to be successful and how to get and use the tools and expertise you need.

PRELIMINARY QUESTIONS

Before figuring out the basic tool kit you'll need to do business in the new economy, there is a series of questions you need to ask about you, your business, your goals, your consumers, and the conditions that permeate your market area. These questions are designed to guide you to a picture of your business that will, in turn, allow you to describe the ideal tool kit.

1. *Yourself.* Begin by determining your level of comfort with technology. There is a high probability that you have and regularly use some sort of computer, and that you have and use an e-mail box. In addition, you probably use a cell phone to remain in touch with your family, friends, colleagues, customers, and clients. In some cases, you may

---

[1] This rule holds for all the businesses of real estate. For agents, the customer referred to is the public; for the broker and the MLS, it's the agent; for the association, it's the broker and the agent.

have additional machines that regulate your daily existence, both personal and business. Ask yourself where you use these tools and how often you rely on each of them. Do the same for the software programs that you use. Which are your favorites? What features are most important to you? For example, if you use a laptop as a major tool, size and weight are probably important to you. If you rely heavily on a personal data assistant (PDA), then functionality will be a criterion for judgment. Doing a personal inventory will allow you to draw a profile of how you use technology and then allow you to set up the most important standards by which you will judge any product that the market presents to you.

2. *Your business.* Survey your business practice. If it is primarily local, if you deal mostly with local properties and local buyers, your communications needs are less than if you have an international practice or deal in a second home market where your buyers are located at some distance. In general, sophistication increases with distance, both for the principal and for the agent. Your tool kit must reflect this.

3. *Your goals.* Figure out what you really want to be when you grow up. At the end of the last chapter, we discussed the need for strategic thinking. That entails formulating a long-term goal and then choosing paths that will take you there. This must be in place before you can choose the tools that will carry you there. Your tool kit is highly results-sensitive. It will reward you to spend a significant amount of time formulating your strategies.

4. *Your customers.* Business success in the new economy is inexorably linked to knowledge of the customer base. It is especially crucial to understand how your customers want to receive information, what information they wish to receive, and what services they expect of you. In fact, there is nothing more important to achieving success in the new economy. Leaving a voice message for a customer who expects to be contacted via e-mail can end a business relationship. Most real estate professionals grew up in a business where they called the tune. In the new economy, the consumer determines how, where, and when business

will be done. You need to, in the words of Tony Soprano, "respect the bing."

5. *Market conditions.* In the first chapter, we discussed the fall of the technology start-ups. It is interesting but understandable why most of these companies began in the San Francisco Bay area. For our purposes, the important point is that this market area contained a great number of technologically sophisticated consumers who understood and were comfortable with information technology. That provided a ready market for companies seeking to leverage new products and systems. It is inconceivable (with no disrespect intended) that the Silicon Valley culture could ever have originated in Allentown, Pennsylvania. The conditions in your market will affect the tools you use to address that market. Just as consumers exhibit varying levels of technological sophistication, so do market areas. And the character of the market in which you operate will affect the tools you need to bring to the marketplace. Find out as much as you can about the industries active in your market area, the types of jobs they need, and the dynamics of industry and population movements. Let this information shape the tool kit you bring to work.

THE BASIC SETUP

There are two basic rules governing the tools you use. First, *understand the results you are trying to accomplish before you select your tools.* A hammer may be excellent for driving nails, but miserable for cutting wood. Until you inventory your needs by asking the questions posed above and until you set down a business plan like the one found in the Appendix, you can't begin to figure out the level of technology you need.

The second rule is that *you must be as sophisticated as your most sophisticated customer yet able to communicate with everyone in a manner that is understood.* Consumers are constantly being educated by other businesses, by the media, and by their children as to how technology can benefit them. Yet, they absorb these lessons to different degrees and with different speeds. Not everyone with whom you deal will have DSL or T-1 lines in their home, or even where they work, but some will. Not everyone will use a wireless modem embedded in a PDA to communicate, but some will. You need to be prepared not only to show your competence to the most advanced of your customers and clients but also to be able to hold the hands of the more technophobic.

That said, the tools you will be using can be roughly divided into three categories: *communications, information management,* and *personal (or business) management.* The importance of each of these will vary, based on the business involved. For agents, personal management is far more important than it is to brokers[2] or the MLS. Similarly, information management is central and probably more important than it is for the agent. The one certain thing is that communications tools are primary for all of the businesses of real estate.

COMMUNICATIONS

Because real estate is a business of people and information and because the technological revolution that has produced the new economy has centered around communications, we start here. In using old tools, real estate professionals have usually been attentive to developing and maintaining communication links. This has been done through the telephone, whether in the office or mobile. It was an effective, though lengthy, process and more importantly met the expectations of consumers.

Now the communications bar has been raised. The telephone, even mobile, has ceased to be the communication device of choice for most consumers. E-mail is faster, more direct, and more efficient. In many cases it's also cheaper.

Exchanges of information and views that had previously occupied voice lines now occupy data lines. All this means that you need to rely on e-mail as your primary form of communication with your clients and customers. That in turn means treating e-mail as you would your telephone. You would not think of checking on your phone messages only once a day. Yet, many real estate professionals seem to feel that only an occasional glance at

---

[2] The exception here is the brokerage operating under a model in which the agent is the primary customer. See Chapter 6 for a discussion.

the e-mail will be sufficient to maintain adequate communication with customers and brokers.

A story will make the point. Jim Sherry, a colleague of mine and one of the brightest thinkers in the real estate industry, was faced with a dilemma. He had put his house on sale and got a surprisingly rapid offer. The offer was attractive but carried with it the stipulation that he move out of the house within ten days. This proved a problem, as he had not yet found another house to move into. Moreover, his schedule was such that he could not devote full time and attention to the move.

The answer came from his agent. In a blinding series of e-mails that crossed the country from Florida to California to Virginia, the agent located possible homes, e-mailed the descriptions and pictures of the homes, and executed a contract on a new house that would be available in the specified time frame. The entire process was done without face-to-face contact and only two telephone calls. The result was more than satisfactory and the move occurred smoothly.

Could this have happened with other tools? Yes, but the need for speed and the distances that separated principal and agent dictated the use of modern electronic communications technology. Notice that with fairly ordinary communications tools, the deal was done, and done while the principals were widely separated.

Your communications tools are the most important investment you can make. At the least, you should have an easily remembered e-mail address that can be checked several times a day. If you are always on the move, a PDA device, such as the Blackberry, that can be used with a wireless modem is a must. In any case, because the expectations of your clients and customers are that you will be available on their timetable,[3] you need to be there or be an inferior choice in the marketplace.

Beyond e-mail, the next most important communications device you can have is a prominent, easily remembered and

---

[3] In some cases, the expectations are reinforced by the brokerage community. Many large firms are directing leads to agents via e-mail, but only for a time. If the agent does not respond to the lead within a few hours, the lead goes to another agent who will respond. More on this in Chapter 6.

well-publicized web site. Here are the basic guidelines to follow in developing your web site:

- *Use expertise, but only that which you can trust.* There are lot of free services out there that will set up your Web site for free and maintain it for you. Some are good, some are not. The economists' adage, "There's no such thing as a free lunch," applies here. Even if you have to use your teenager's grungy friends, make sure that the Web master you choose is someone you know and can rely on to be there when you need help.
- *Make people want to go back there again and again.* Static sites repel visitors. If you go back to a site for the second time and nothing has changed, you will never return. Make your site lively and interesting, and change it often (not just the listings on it, but the content). Include information that consumers will find valuable about their local area and about homeownership. Link your site to others that attract visitors, so that they can use your site as a channel to the rest of the world. To see how this is done at the broker level, visit the Baird and Warner site (www.bairdand-warner.com), which shows how a company can create a site that has power and creativity. For an individual site, check out www.terrimurphy.com, where content equals attractiveness.[4]
- *Publicize the site to death.* Everywhere your name appears, link it to your Web address. The majority of consumers are led to a site in two ways: either they see the URL advertised or they assume the business they seek has one under its name and search for it. Without publicity, your site will lie dormant, no matter how good and meaty it is.
- *Create a number of Web paths to your door.* Your site will be the primary vehicle for your Web presence, but there are other ways of allowing the consumer to reach you. The most obvious are Microsoft's Home Advisor, realtor.com, and your company site. All will allow the home seeker access to you.

---

[4] Also see Terry Murphy's book, *e-listing and e-selling secrets,* Chicago: Real Estate Education Company, 2001. It is a treasury of useful informati   ' '' how to operate the agent business in the new economy.

But there are other, more local, and more targeted ways to attract business. E-neighbors (www.eneighbors.com) is a company that creates community Web sites for areas as specific as a subdivision. By sponsoring the neighborhoods that constitute your market area, you can frame local news of great interest to consumers with your name and your Web address. Other opportunities also exist. Seek them out.

- *The only bad Web site is the nonexistent one.* Technological paralysis is the enemy of business success in the new economy. You can't win the lottery unless you buy a ticket. Don't have a Web site? Get one—*now!*

These guidelines represent the basics. At a more advanced level, your Web site can be equipped to show property using streaming video. Visitors will be able to get a much better feel for what your listings actually represent and they'll have fun doing it. Additionally, advanced Web technology will allow you to create interactive relationships with visitors to determine their needs and preferences, as well as capture their Web addresses for later follow-up. At this stage, you have exceeded your individual expertise. Advanced Web adventures should only be done under the supervision of a technology professional.

INFORMATION MANAGEMENT

Somewhere during the typical listing presentation, the real estate professional hits a wall. It occurs when the client asks how the agent will specifically market the property. The answer is the recitation of the usual outlets (newspapers, TV, and now the Internet) through which property has always been marketed. High-end properties will command their own glossy brochures and presentations in a selected list of publications perused by wealthy potential buyers, but the run-of-the-mill property will get run-of-the-mill treatment.

That doesn't cut it anymore in the new economy. Data management techniques are sufficiently developed so that consumers can be specifically targeted to the point that each feels he or she is the only customer. If you can't do the same with their property needs, you will be seen as an inferior choice in the marketplace. You can avoid the listing wall by using information management techniques and tools. Your marketing of property must include a demonstration that you understand the features of the property, the audiences that would be most interested in the property, where that audience can be found, and how it can be reached.[5]

So, after communications, the next set of tools to look at is that bearing on the assembly, management, and presentation of information. At the most basic level, you need to be able to create and present electronic listing presentations. This means becoming familiar with a laptop computer equipped with video and audio capabilities, a CD drive, and sufficient memory to handle a multimedia presentation.

For sellers, you will use the laptop to create a listing presentation that will be in effect a video brochure for the property. This includes pictures of the house and its rooms (preferably full views that move), and information on the location of the property, including neighborhood characteristics, commuting patterns, and the location of essential services. It will also show economic profiles of the most likely buyers and their locations. The final element is the marketing plan you will use to sell the property.

For buyers, the package may consist of several home "brochures." Each concentrates on the description and the setting of the property. The purpose is to allow the potential buyer to prescreen houses and thus save time and other resources that might otherwise be wasted in a long search. Creating a compact or floppy disc with all the home brochures in which the customer is interested and labeled with your contact information not only customizes the home search but also identifies you as the source of that customization. This becomes a value-added service that plays well in the new economy.

On a more advanced level, you can use all the information that real estate professionals capture to create detailed market-

---

[5] This requires what is generally referred to as "data mining" and usually requires considerable expertise. In the agent business, this expertise must be leased; in the broker business, it should be part of the competency of the firm; in the MLS business, it is an absolute prerequisite; in the association business, it is unnecessary.

for every one of your clients. REALTORS® collect detailed
ation on each potential homebuyer with whom they work.
This includes demographic and personal information as well as
financial data unavailable to few other businesses. Yet once the
buyer is qualified in a specific price range, the information is
often discarded. In a full data-mining operation, the information
would be blended with public databases (primarily the U.S.
Census) to identify and target high-probability buyers for specific properties.

Doing this requires forming a strategic partnership with a
database professional who can find and manipulate the information. You bring to the partnership an understanding of what end
result is needed to provide superior service to your clients in
marketing their properties. These professionals can be found
most easily at your local college or university, but with the collapse of the dot-coms, it's a buyers' market for techies.

The other major topic in the area of information management has to do with broker reciprocity. This process, by which all
MLS listings appear on each individual broker's site in a given
market, has grown quickly. In some markets, such as Seattle
(where the process originated), reciprocity has been driven by
large brokers; in others, such as Houston (where the market is
more diversified), it has been driven by the local association. In
January 2002, NAR released writing guidelines to govern reciprocity in all markets.

The free exchange of information between firms and its provision to the public through public Web sites can equalize market
leverage among competitors. Now, the ability to attract the consumer does not depend on the number of listings the firms has,
but rather on the overall attractiveness of the site and the additional content it contains. While this still gives the advantage to
larger firms, it opens up the field to all companies.

Oddly enough, given the role of NAR in broker reciprocity,
the major casualty of the exchange of information on brokers'
sites may well be realtor.com. When the program is fully operational, local sites will be as powerful as any national site. Given
the greater name recognition of local firms such as Long and
Foster in the Washington, D.C. area and Windermere and John
L. Scott in Seattle, traffic is likely to move to them rather than to
realtor.com. They will also be more current, loading MLS infor-

mation in real time without the lag of the national site. Scott found in a research study that 60 percent of home buyers in the Northwest used the Internet, and 57 percent of these went to the John L. Scott site, but only 12 percent visited realtor.com.[6]

The need here is the information management tools to keep your company site vital and interesting to the public, while at the same time capturing leads that are generated as consumers visit the site. Every time a consumer lands on your site, the information generated can ultimately result in a listing or sale. But this happens only if you're set up to capture the details of the visit. Marketing professionals in other industries are far ahead of real estate in this regard. There are lessons to be learned from looking at how they do it and how it can apply to real estate. This is another case where professional talent, either on staff or outsourced, is necessary.

PERSONAL BUSINESS MANAGEMENT

Real estate professionals are among the most organized of all businesspeople. Given the amount of information they need to juggle, this is hardly surprising; the unorganized quickly fall by the wayside. New information technology has created the ability to handle huge amounts of information, and with this it has had its most significant impact on the real estate business.

Traditionally, real estate has been a labor-intensive business. Communication and transaction management have been accomplished by physical means, whether by the real estate firm, the agent, or a personal assistant. The automobile has been such a valuable tool in the real estate practice simply because of the need to physically transport people and papers to different sites. The result has been a severe strain on the real estate professional's time and a resulting lack of life balance.

Personal management tools have gradually seeped into real estate, starting most probably with the mobile phone. This allowed for business to be done quickly from anywhere with little

---

[6] Kevin Hawkins, "Broker Reciprocity," *Real Estate Technology,* summer 2001, p. 18. These numbers are consistent with the CAR survey described in Chapter 2.

loss of efficiency. To understand how important the mobile phone is to the business, see what happens at breaks in meetings of Realtors. The phones pop out and messages are scrawled, while the bank of pay phones, once nearly fought over, remains silent and empty.[7]

And it goes farther. It is now a minimal requirement that real estate professionals have a mobile phone with voice messaging, caller ID, and call waiting. This is accompanied by a digital pager to allow for consumer access at any time. At a slightly higher level, PDAs like Palms and Blackberry have superseded the old Daytimers and Rolodexes as schedule keepers of choice. They will hold your address book and your calendar and can relay e-mail.

On the business side, there is a constellation of software available to allow you to keep your prospects and listings in order. Top Producer is the dean of these programs, but increasingly has competition from other quarters. Some brokers (see Chapter 6) are bundling personal management services and marketing them to agents as a business model. The availability and effectiveness of the technology allows this to happen.

EDUCATION AND TRAINING

The real estate market is a more challenging place; the old tools and skills will no longer hack it. But it takes more than just tools; you need to acquire the training you need in order to exercise the skills. That training will differ from individual to individual, depending on their current skill and awareness of technology. Thus, it must be customized to be completely useful. Luckily, current information technology allows for customization. More importantly, it allows for the content to be adjusted to the level of the participants, thus eliminating the "least common denominator" effect that plagues real estate continuing education.

---

[7] Yet another casualty of the new economy, pay phones are owned either by regional telephone companies (the "Baby Bells") or by private firms. Before cell phones, this was very profitable business; it is now marginal at best.

The most promising and most important impact of technology on training is the capacity for distance learning. Essentially, this means receiving training at a physical location different from the point of instruction. Initially, distance learning was delivered through videotapes, sometimes broadcast over private networks, as Re/Max has done for years.

While this channel remains viable and, in fact, is the delivery system of choice for most distance learners, it is being superseded by the Internet. With its economy, ease of delivery, and pull technology (allowing receivers to pick and choose what they want individually), the Internet will eventually allow any individual to access a Harvard-level education affordably and conveniently.[8] Information technology increasingly allows the updating of course material quickly and easily.

In the real estate business, all the franchises have or will attempt to develop distance learning through the Internet. Clearly the bandwidth factor (of both the cabling system and the real estate professional) will determine the ability of distance learning to reach the majority of real estate professionals. But the delivery system must serve as a channel for relevant material. For the most part, real estate education needs to be more content-rich; the new marketplace demands new skills.

The biggest hole in the area of real estate management is education for the office manager. Current practice is that the firm creates managers from salespeople who are either very successful or very unsuccessful. They receive very little training in management and usually remain as salespeople. In addition, office managers report to owners or regional managers who are unprepared for the challenge of training management so that they have the tools to solve problems. This is a recipe for mediocrity or failure. The firm cannot rely on the managers to execute the chosen strategies, and the managers are not fully capable of dealing with a group of independent contractors.

Right now, the distance-learning business is full of vendors. Eventually, the field will consolidate around several high-quality, well-funded, highly competent providers. The most apt analogy is

---

[8] Which, of course, raises a problem for midlevel universities that feature high prices and middling education. Their fate may well be that of the travel agents who lost 40 percent of their business to the Internet.

e sorting out of the auto industry in the first quarter of
entury, when the number of companies went from hun-
just three. For now, though, look at www.isucceed.com.
online storehouse of techniques and materials that can be
ac. sed when you need to use them. In addition, you might want
to join the Real Estate Cyberspace Society (www.Recyber.com); it
provides monthly tips on gathering the best information and techniques from the Internet, as well as interviews and tips from real
estate gurus.

As distance learning grows, the traditional methods of real
estate education will have to change. In particular, as continuing
education is delivered online, it must be accompanied by some
form of testing to allow the sanctioning body to certify and ver-
ify the student. This is not the case now, as mere attendance is
sufficient to receive continuing education credit. These are issues that prelicense and continuing education regulators are
going to have to wrestle with.

A FINAL WORD

The one discussion missing from this chapter is that of a
transaction-management system. Three years ago, it appeared
that the industry was on the verge of developing and introducing
an integrated system that would fully automate the real estate
firm's "back room." In fact, it appeared that several competing
systems were about to hit the street. This has not been the case,
and the transaction-management system is the virtual reality of
the real estate business—all promise and no delivery.

Right now, the industry is no closer to a workable transaction-management system than it was three years ago. The efforts
that have come close have failed, usually because of lack of capital, and those that have succeeded have been fairly simple and
not capable of expansion. Many more have been pure vaporware,
systems that were trumpeted and then found to be only concepts,
several years away from fruition. For now, you can watch the development of transaction-management systems from a distance,
knowing that you will someday be using them. For now, ignore
the claims that the future is here.

One Agent's Tool Kit

These are the tools used by Wynne Achatz, Real Estate One Westrick Associates, Marine City, Mich., a sophisticated, high-producing agent.

- **Hardware**
  HP Laser Jet 4L (Black and white)
  Epson Stylus 740 (color)
  HP Color Desk Jet
  Dell Inspirion 7500 with docking station
  Gateway Desktop
  NEC 120L (for travel)
  Kodak 280 Digital Camera
  Nokia digital (with headset)
  Stereo microphone
  HP CapShare portable scanner

- **Generic Software**
  Microsoft: Front Page 2000, Word, Excel, Publisher,
    Outlook, IE5
  Quick Books
  Backup to Advantage Technologies system
  Norton Anti-virus
  ArcaMax

- **Free Software**
  Adobe Acrobat Reader
  Free Fax (www.faxwave.com)
  Hotsend (www.hotsend.com)
  Gator
  GuruNet (www.GuruNet.com)
  www.Freei.com

- **Real Estate Software**
  Top Producer
  Palm V with Supra Key Reader
  PREP Real Suite
  Vista Info Rexplorer MLS
  IPIX
  Virtual Tours.com
  ENeighborhood personal edition
  Express Copy Quik Linx
  World Merge
  Zip Forms

This list represents a solid, well-considered tool kit. The problem is that there is yet no single utility that can link all the pieces together into a single system. This will be the next great development in real estate technology.

Chapter 6

The New World of Real Estate Brokerage

MONEY ON THE TABLE

Since Re/Max popularized the 100 percent concept in the early 1970s, the function of brokerage has been steadily eroded as a viable business model. Company dollar has declined, and brokers who were not selling on their own or who did not own related businesses that could generate ancillary income gradually have disappeared. Real estate has become an agent's business, not a broker's. The broker has been trapped by this because the prevailing philosophy of business has been that the more agents you have, the more money you make; even if the agent keeps, on average, 70 percent of the commission, that still leaves 30 percent to cover expenses and generate a profit.[1]

The reaction by most brokers of any significant size and market share has been to attempt to control other parts of the settlement process. Thus, they have bought, created, or partnered with mortgage companies, title companies and home

---

[1] This is less wise than it seems. Nearly 50 percent of all REALTORS® (not to mention all licensees) produce nothing either for themselves or for the firm in any given year.

inspectors to drive those parts of the transactions toward them. Yet, success was limited, because agents, being independent contractors, saw no particular obligation to use the companies or relationships controlled by the broker. Agents did what was in their own best interests. Recently, with the increased need for technology by agents, some brokerages have instituted "technology" fees, levied on the agents on a monthly basis and generating not only revenues but also profits for the broker. A variation on this theme is the transaction fee, due on settlement, that is the responsibility of the agent but is most often paid by the buyer.

All these measures represent broker reaction to the reality of the market when seen through the filter of conventional wisdom. These are the only ways in which the broker can make up for the decline in company dollar occasioned by the increasing commission share claimed by agents. But if the conventional wisdom is discarded and the entire customer relationship examined with new eyes, another potential revenue source (or set of revenue sources) emerges. Right now, the agent engages a consumer when that consumer chooses to enter the real estate market as either buyer or seller, and then takes that consumer through the entire transaction process. This involves helping the buyer sort through available properties; helping the seller prepare the property for sale; preparing and negotiating a contract; and arranging for financing, inspection, title clearance, and finally, settlement.

At that point the agent leaves the consumer with a parting gift and turns his or her attention to the next consumer ready to enter the market. While the agent may send an annual gift (usually a calendar) or the occasional postcard, the closing of the property usually signals the end of the relationship. The best agents keep a cadre of customers who return frequently, but the average agent moves from deal to deal rather than keeping the customer for life. If you open up the real estate ownership process, the word *life* has real meaning for the bottom line. Consider Figure 6-1, a depiction of the cycle the typical household goes through from purchase to sale of a property.[2] The degree to which that household uses property-related services

---

[2] I am indebted to Ari Vidali, Chief Technical Officer of iProperty.com, for this diagram.

after the closing of the sale is actually greater than before th (even if we include moving as part of the closing process).

The potential revenue from the customer relationship expands after the sale. The "move and improve" stage encompasses all the changes that the household wishes to make to the property in order to make it a home. The home also is a place, and the need for the household to establish itself as part of that place will generate another set of "homeownership and community" services. Finally, the household will reenter the real estate market, usually as both a seller and a buyer. This entire stage of the relationship with the consumer is, in effect, money left on the table by the real estate firm.

FIGURE 6.1 One Stop Shopping

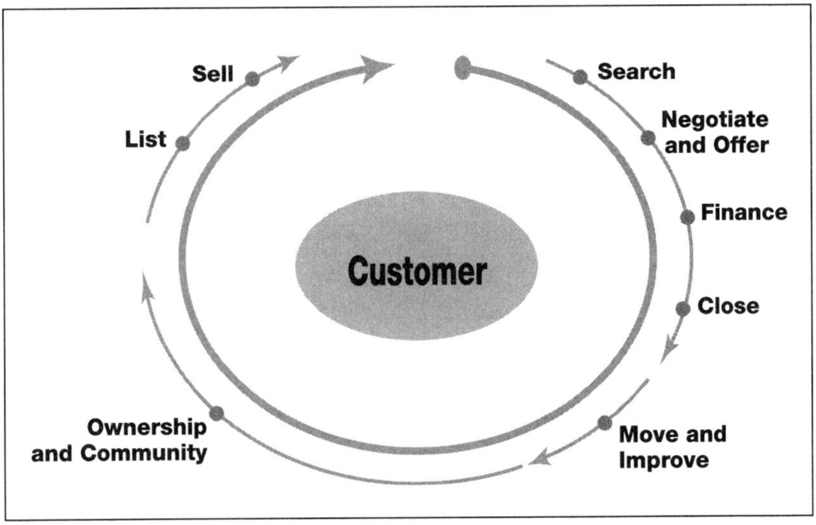

CAPTURING REVENUES

The challenge to the broker-owner is to find ways to capture the revenues that are available in the marketplace. Those that are attempting to do so are pursuing one or more of three different models for real estate brokerage:

1. *Extension of services:* The brokerage attempts to reclaim the money left on the table by extending the aftercare services it provides to consumers. The broker attempts to position the firm as the first point of contact for consumers when-

ever they need any product or service to fill their home ownership needs. The company's revenues come from brokering these services to households.

2. *Direct to the consumer:* The brokerage recruits and services customers directly, rather than relying on an agent sales force. Services may be offered in a package (as is standard in the industry) or on a fee-for-service, menu-based system. The companies using this model extensively tend to be new in the business and thus don't need to eradicate conventional wisdom before proceeding. They also tend to use salaried agents (who may or may not be employees) rather than a commission-based sales force. Revenues are derived from capturing as much of the transaction for the company as possible.

3. *Servicing the agent:* The brokerage sees the agent as its primary customer and seeks to create a technological "cocoon" that allows the agent to be as successful as possible in the new economy. This includes lead generation, client management, and transaction service, as well as all the personal business services needed by the agent. The company derives revenues by leasing the technology to the agents, usually at a monthly fee.[3]

These three models are not mutually exclusive, and some companies combine them, usually integrating the extension-of-services model with one of the other two. More significantly, larger companies may seek to use a range of models within a single organization, as Coldwell Banker has done with its Blue Edge approach. The reasoning here is that consumers who think their transactions should be handled a certain way (e.g., for-sale-by-owner) may find later that they need a different approach. Having a variety of models within a single company will retain customers even if the service changes. As one large broker said to me, "There can be many doors, as long as it's my house."

The introduction of new models for brokerage hinges on a major change in the current business. Right now, the agent

---

[3] This differs from the technology fee mentioned earlier because it represents payment for real services rather than the provision of some generalized notion of "technology."

"owns" the consumer. The agent recruits the consumer, cultivates the consumer, brings the consumer into the market, and ultimately guides the closing of the deal. The broker enters the picture only at the point of contract when his or her signature needs to be on the document. At that point, the records of the transaction and the information available on the consumer are available to the broker.

Clearly, to implement new models, the broker needs more connection with the consumer, both at an earlier stage of the process and in a much more intensive way. In the direct-to-the-consumer model the path to this relationship is obvious; in fact, the need for the broker to control the customer is one of the motivating factors in moving to this model. But for the others, a deal must be struck. Ultimately, given the need of the broker for more contact with the consumer and the need of the agent for more and better tools to use in the business, a deal will be struck: In return for access to the customer earlier and more frequently, the broker will undertake the cost of buying or building the necessary technology for the agent to use.

This chapter describes in detail each of the new models of real estate brokerage. All three of them are in the market now, along with hybrids that combine models. The descriptions will thus be descriptions of work in progress rather than theory. Additionally, we take a look at where the brokerage business is going in a macro sense, i.e., where consolidation and cross-industry mergers might lead the market. If you are a small broker, this chapter will help you think through the value proposition you wish to present to the marketplace in the new economy. The longer you have been in business, the less likely it is that you have changed your operations to reflect the new models and the more you will benefit from an understanding of the new models. If you are a large broker, you are probably already pursuing one or more of these models. This chapter will give you a bit of a reality check and perhaps spark some thinking on the next stage of development you wish to implement.

NSION OF SERVICES

ɪ nis model is quite simple and is illustrated best in Figure 6-1. It involves the provision of services for the household after the sale so that the new owners can have easy access to reliable vendors from a single point of contact and the real estate firm can be seen as the primary provider of care for the household. The firm gains a customer for life while generating an ancillary revenue stream from the relationship with vendors. When the household is ready to enter the market as seller and/or buyer, the firm it chooses will be the one that has served its homeownership needs over the years.

Some extension of services has been the classic reaction of the real estate owner-broker to the loss of commission dollars to agents. Traditionally, this has taken place within the context of the real estate transaction itself and has most often encompassed title insurance and mortgage origination. Virtually all of the 500 largest real estate firms either own a mortgage company or have a tight working relationship with one. Many own their own title companies.

The economics of these arrangements make great sense. In a normal market, given the average commission split, the broker makes about $125 from each residential real estate transaction. Each mortgage origination will yield about $1,000. The breakeven point is thus one transaction out of eight: If the broker can place every eighth transaction in which the company is involved with his or her mortgage company, then the mortgage business will yield as much revenue as the brokerage business. The industry average is closer to one in five, which means that the mortgage business is more lucrative than is the brokerage business.[4]

It pays the broker to spend more time and other resources on developing the mortgage business and to generate as many transactions as possible by maximizing the numbers of agents on the street. This can also mean attracting the highest producers by offering not only all of the commission but also additional benefits that actually bring the broker's cost of having a top producer to

---

[4] Consider how this relates to the example of Chrysler described in Chapter 4. You need to know what business you're in.

more than the revenue generated. In many cases, then, b
age is a kind of loss leader, important only to bring in co
for a profitable mortgage origination business. Title insurance
carries an even larger margin, suggesting the same approach.

It is a small step from this to a full extension of services.
These services will of necessity extend beyond the closing on the
property because this is territory where the new buyer feels concern and the need for assistance and where agents have not yet
ventured. In the words of Chip Roach, chairman of Prudential
Fox Roach, "We need a business model to add more value [for
our customers] so we can prove the cost of our services is worth-
while. We need to develop multifaceted relationships with people
after the sale to get more business." *The purpose is to create a customer for life, not just for the transaction.*

The difference between these extensions and those contained within the real estate transaction itself is the difference
between *build* and *buy.* It is generally easy for a real estate firm to
enter the mortgage brokerage or title business. Licenses are easy
to get, capital requirements low, and familiarity with potential
employees high. In addition, brokers have dealt with the mortgage and title processes regularly for years as an adjunct to their
dealings with buyers and sellers.

With other extensions, however, experience on the part of
the real estate company is lacking. Moving, home improvement
and renovation, landscaping, and all the other things that per-
sonalize a house and turn it into a home have always been
defined as belonging to another world, not to real estate. Yet, the
attractiveness of a single point of contact for these services is as
great for the household as any other kind of one-stop shopping,
including that for real estate transaction services.

The initial attempts to extend services began locally, with individual companies striking agreements with local trades, who
would be "preferred providers." Thus, particular moving companies, locksmiths, painters, and landscapers would be referenced
and promoted in any materials the company shared with its customers. There would be a fee for the promotion and an
additional referral fee for any business originating from the relationship. Thus, the company had two types of revenue streams:
the original signup fee and the continuing flow of referrals.

One of the most successful of these programs was the one
developed by Long and Foster, the real estate giant in the Mid-

Atlantic region. It was essentially designed as a referral system in which the company served as the introduction point between vendor and customer, although the customer saw the service as being delivered from Long and Foster. As described by Manny Garcia, who created the program for Long and Foster:

> Our program was based on being able to get clients for the vendor before, during and after the transaction. The idea was based on getting clients for life rather than getting more current clients. In our first year we had over 25,000 individual users visiting the site over 300,000 times with an average user session length of 38 minutes and 11 seconds. The clients were using the system and they were buying from the vendors. We made great strides in developing this program and realized to reap greater rewards we needed more than a web-based business model. We needed live operators to make this work by increasing the sales to the vendors from the clients.[5]

There are some interesting lessons here. First, local knowledge can drive business. The advantage that brokers have in understanding their market areas can create a more effective program by confining that program to vendors they know to be reliable and competent. Second, electronic connection is not enough. These programs need to be sold in the old-fashioned way, with people contacting people.

Another manifestation of the extension-of-service model is the concierge-type program. These programs provide a link between the consumer and the vendor, but they also arrange for necessary services for new homeowners, including address changes, utility hookups, and all the other time-consuming changes that have to be made to successfully move from one location to another. These programs have worked well on the local level, but less so nationally. The most prominent national program was the one administered by Coldwell Banker. Conceived to provide service to the current purchasers and sellers of the

---

[5] Long and Foster dropped its program and joined the Home Link system in 2000. They saw the need to increase the program usage by their clients and thought they had gone as far as possible with the web mode.

local franchises, it did not provide enough depth with local vendors to attract enough usage. The franchisees had to alter the program locally to be able to attract vendors by including past clients. Otherwise, there was not much incentive for the vendors to join a program that would at best be able to provide less than 5,000 leads in large metropolitan markets. Real estate companies also balked at the need to pay a fee for the program and then recruit the local vendors themselves.

The national-local dilemma is the single most significant obstacle to the implementation of the extension-of-services model. Because real estate is essentially local, the relationships with vendors have to be rooted in the local market. If a national franchise, for example, signs a contract with Merry Maids to offer a discounted home-cleaning service to its customers, that contract will have no attraction for either the franchisee or the homeowner if the service is not available locally.[6] Yet, the economics of the model require that profit come only through scale: If you are not big enough to recruit and maintain a system of vendors locally, you cannot offer full service to the household.

The solution to this has come into the market through a company called Home Link, established in Connecticut by Bill Raveis and now in use by a number of real estate firms throughout the country. In the Home Link system, the programs are administered out of a central point, which also provides software to link customers and vendors, national advertising, and promotion. Each individual company enrolls vendors in its own market areas, and charges them fees consistent with the level of promotion they will receive. The services provided are at the discretion of the local company and the local relationships are retained. In essence, Home Link is a way to reap the economies of scale of a national company without sacrificing the local relationships that are at the heart of the real estate business.

Given the consumer predilection for one-stop shopping and the way in which technology has increased the speed and effi-

---

[6] This concept was hammered home to me quickly when I joined the staff of the National Association of REALTORS®. Figuring that REALTOR® bought a lot of printing, I floated the idea of a national print contract as a way of saving money for the members. The idea was quickly scotched, on the grounds that REALTORS® wanted as many local ties as possible to promote business referrals and therefore wanted to deal only with their local printers.

ciency of connectivity, some extension of services is a necessity for the real estate brokerage. The real questions are how and how far this will proceed. The "how" question has been largely answered. Whether it is through a national comprehensive program like Home Link, a purely local system like those maintained by some large firms, or the use of individual companies (for example, Mover Link connects consumers and moving companies to take care of that single need), there are mechanisms available for firms of all sizes to extend the services they offer consumers.

The "how far" question is up in the air. Right now, REALTORS® are concerned about the entrance of banks into the real estate business. They feel that the size and market power of the banks will overwhelm what is essentially an industry of small businesses. Yet, real estate professionals deal with consumers in an intimate way when their most sensitive financial decisions are being made. It's as easy to conceive of real estate firms offering financial planning and advisory services to households as it is to imagine banks entering the real estate industry. Whether this happens or not, the extension-of-service model in some form will be part of the operations of every real estate firm that succeeds in the new economy.

DIRECT TO THE CONSUMER

The direct-to-the-consumer model is most closely associated now with the electronic real estate start-up companies that in the past three years have entered the market. Their value proposition to consumers is that they will provide the same set of services as all other companies, but at a lower price because they use the Internet and e-mail to streamline the process. Lower costs passed on to the consumer have always been a siren song of business, and this one has a new-economy twist to it. But the guts of the model are that the firm generates business through advertising, then executes the business using licensees who are largely salaried.

Traditionally, the real estate firm acquires customers through a sales force, agents who farm territories to discover likely buyers and sellers whom they then bring to the firm when a transaction is likely. At any point, the firm is unaware, except in a very general sense, of who its customers are. This is very different from the way in which most businesses operate and stems from the independent contractor relationship between the broker and the agent. The only exceptions to this model have been the limited service firms that performed some essential services for sellers who wanted to be their own agents.

Some large firms have had a direct link to the public through toll-free numbers advertised in local media. These occasionally resulted in leads that were then referred to agents. In some cases, the agents were employed by the firm and were on salary. This part of the business has grown recently, spurred by the widespread use of the Internet. We discuss it further below.

The first real introduction of the direct-to-the-consumer model came in 1999 with the inception of Zip Realty and eRealty, followed later by Your Home Direct. All of these leveraged the Internet and used electronic communication extensively to reduce the labor content of their business. With listings online, electronic links to mortgage and title companies, and the familiarity of the public in dealing with information electronically, it made sense (at least in theory) to service a larger number of customers with fewer real estate professionals.

These firms (Zip Realty in the San Francisco Bay area, eRealty in Houston and Austin, Your Home Direct in New Jersey[7]) began operations in markets where the populations were technologically sophisticated and where home prices were high. The value proposition they presented to the market traded on these two characteristics. Their systems were the hip new ways of doing real estate; they could offer listing and sales services for a smaller dollar figure than could conventional real estate companies.[8]

---

[7] Another variant, SOMA Living Center, may seem to belong in this group, and in fact antecedes them all. But SOMA is meant to provide limited service to buyers and in that sense is more akin to the limited referral offices maintained by many East coast firms, rather than the newer direct-to-the-consumer models.

[8] These companies are not essentially discount brokerages. Rather, they have reconceived the way in which the transaction process takes place and have driven down its cost. They then pass this cost saving through to the consumer. They are demonstrating the truism that it takes just as much effort to sell a low-priced house as a high-priced one, and therefore the fees charged should be about equal.

While none of these companies has attained significant market share anywhere, they have been successful enough to show the rest of the industry that some new ways of doing business may be in order. In doing so, they have spawned two significant developments. The first of these is the foray of Coldwell Banker into the direct-to-the-consumer market through its new Blue Edge Realty. This is a limited experiment (in Pittsburgh, PA, and Springfield, IL), designed to offer consumers an alternative without losing them to competitors.

While using electronic tools to streamline the transaction, the Blue Edge system allows consumers to choose the services they wish to buy from the real estate firm and charges accordingly. In this, Blue Edge is a bit closer to the traditional for-sale-by-owner companies than it is to Zip and the others. Right now, it's just an experiment, but it is clear that the proof of concept provided by Zip, eRealty, and Your Home Direct has moved a large national company to look at other models. Coldwell Banker's experience may well prod other established firms to look at these as well.

The second significant development of the direct-to-the-consumer model is the increased emphasis traditional firms are placing on generating leads through the company rather than through the agents. Virtually every large independent company now uses its promotional activities, particularly its Web site, to drive consumers directly to the company. This has been facilitated by broker reciprocity, which has enabled all companies in a given MLS to populate their sites with all the listings on the MLS. By advertising this, they offer the consumer the convenience of one-stop shopping for the property. By promoting the company, they get the leads directly.

With the leads, the company can get to know its customers and control their relationship with the brokerage. The leads can be sent to agents on some sort of rotating system (we discuss this later in connection with the servicing-the-agent model), given to in-house salaried agents, or kept and cultivated until the household is ready to buy and then transferred to an agent.[9] The point is that the firm is servicing the customer first and thus has "ownership." This makes service extensions much easier.

---

[9] As Baird and Warner in Chicago is doing quite successfully.

The development of a direct-to-the-consumer model is best when associated with something new. In the case of the electronic real estate firms and Blue Edge, it was a new operation. In the case of the direct appeal to the public by traditional firms, it was associated with a Web presence and broker reciprocity. Short of these, there is little incentive to switch over. A traditional real estate brokerage that relies on "feet on the street" will likely alienate its sales force if it mixes operations.

Newness allows for another element of the direct-to-the-consumer model that is critical to success. This model cannot be implemented using veteran real estate managers and agents. The thought processes that need to be associated with the new model are very different from those of the traditional model. Blue Edge began with new personnel; in the case of the electronic companies, agents and managers were either new or carefully screened veterans.

It makes sense for a traditional real estate company to find a direct route to the customer. Among other things, it allows the company to attract a wider range of customers than it can with only one offering (think Marriott and the price points at which it offers accommodations).[10] But any company that seeks to innovate in this way must do it through a clearly separate operation. Unlike the extension-of-services and servicing-the-agent models, this one cannot be mixed and matched with the traditional model.

SERVICING THE AGENT

At the opposite end of the spectrum from the direct-to-the-consumer model is the servicing-the-agent approach. This model is close to the traditional model but leverages technology to make the broker the primary source for all the agent's business needs. This includes client and transaction management services, but also comprises personal business and organization needs. The

---

[10] Price points are commonplace in the hospitality industry, yet virtually unknown in real estate. I can stay at a Marriott for $40 a night or $400 a night. As the consumer, I get the choice and I drive the transaction. In real estate, one price for one set of services is generally the rule.

guiding philosophy of this model is that if the broker can generate revenue by selling the agents the tools they need to succeed
in the new economy, that success becomes frosting on the cake.
Call it the Levi Strauss model: If you sell dungarees and pans to
the gold prospectors, it doesn't matter which ones strike pay
dirt.[11]

The servicing-the-agent model represents a real attitude shift
on the part of the broker. The broker has always provided the
agent with tools for doing business, whether these were training,
information, or promotion. The broker sought to increase the
agent's sales and in doing so increase the revenue for the brokerage. The new model involves the development of
sophisticated tools that meet all the agent's needs and the licensing of these tools to a group of agents who can use them
profitably.

The broker is establishing a revenue stream that is independent of market conditions and also attracting a cadre of agents
who have the most chance for success in the new economy.
Because servicing the agent in an electronic environment requires significant capital outlay, it makes sense only if the costs
are spread over a large number of agents. The servicing-the-agent
model, then, is primarily a large-firm model.

Attracting successful agents is not unlike pleasing customers.
You need to create a value proposition that they find compelling.
Again like consumers, this happens if you save them time and
take away stress. That, in turn, means streamlining their real estate business processes and simplifying their personal business
lives. The first part has always been the focus of the brokerage
and therefore ought to be easy. The extension into the personal
business of the agent is bit more revolutionary.

The real estate business tools that the agent needs can be broken down into listing and selling, marketing and prospecting,
transactions and home service extensions. The system runs
smoothly when all parts are connected. Thus, if the company

---

[11] This actually is an apt analogy for real estate. Fifty percent of all members of NAR make less than $16 an hour, a rate comparable to semiskilled
labor. The vast majority of commissions are earned by about 10 percent of the
industry. While income might be a little more evenly distributed than it was for
the gold miners of the 19th century, the discrepancy is of the same order.
Betting on the success of individual agents is not the path to riches. Selling
them tools is more promising.

maintains a template for the preparation of listing presentations by the agents, the system becomes more valuable if this software is tied into the MLS database, the online photo software database, and the print shop.

Electronic versions of each of these are available in the marketplace. For the large firm, weaving them together into a single system will increase the value to the agent and make the brokerage operate more smoothly. It is a sensible investment in technology.

The personal business software should be designed to allow agents to organize their prospect and lead management processes but also enable them to order business cards and client gifts, schedule training, and receive information about the industry, their firms and their offices. All these items are a regular part of the REALTOR®'s daily business life; simplifying them will create value that will more than justify the licensing fees the broker charges. There are no prepackaged personal business service software programs. They need to be developed from scratch, and that requires a significant investment. Every large firm has some form of agent service package. The most fully developed version of this approach, however, is found in the Web Top program operated by Prudential California Realty. It provides for every need that the agent has in the real estate transaction process, the personal management process, or the prospecting process.

One particular feature of Web Top links this model to the direct-to-the-consumer model. This is a feature that generates leads from the public and then distributes them to the agents. When a lead goes to an agent, that agent has six hours to contact the prospective customer. If the agent fails to do so, the lead is transferred to another agent. This gives the agent an incentive to provide quick and excellent customer service, while identifying the company as the route to that service. If the lead results in a closed sale, the agent pays the company a referral fee.

The servicing-the-agent model has two major virtues. First, it maintains the traditional relationship between the broker and the agent. The broker still supplies the tools the agent needs to do business, charging the agent through commission splits, desk fees, or some other payment. Only now the tools reflect the new technology used in the business and can extend beyond the real estate transaction.

Second, it puts the broker in a more stable business. Becoming a vendor to the agent is a more viable market position than is relying on commission income. It also allows the broker to concentrate on implementing the extension-of-services model. In fact, between the two models, commission income and more can be ceded to the agent if that's what it takes to attract truly productive agents.

The downside of this model is the vulnerability it imposes on the broker. Financially, the creation of the model requires a substantial investment. While this can be mitigated by licensing existing systems, such as Web Top, it remains a significant outlay. More importantly, the broker becomes merely one of a competing class of vendors. The tools the agent needs can be purchased from any of a number of sources. Like all technologies, these tools will become commodities and therefore the province of the lowest-cost provider.

THE STRUCTURE OF THE INDUSTRY IN THE LONG RUN

In the short run, the industry will move toward some combination of these models. Each of them will work in the new economy if carefully implemented and fully backed. But, it's unclear as to whether any of these will exist down the road. The reason here is that the consolidation of the industry will alter the structure to the point where the prevailing models will come from other industries.

Consolidation among large firms suggests that there may ultimately be a relative handful of companies. The forces we described in Chapter 3 will not go away, and they are likely to intensify the amalgamation of real estate. More important, the entrance by banks into the real estate business will bring with it new models of doing business that are more familiar to banks. Those will supersede the new models that are currently evolving.

For small firms (there will be no midsized firms), cooperative models will emerge. The investment needed to move toward new models of the firm are beyond the means of any one company, but could be affordable by groups of firms, just as agricultural co-ops enabled farmers to adapt to new methods of farming. In that case, these new models will be preserved, particularly the extension-of-services model, because that model preserves the personal service that is the hallmark of the smaller niche firms.

Chapter 7

The Agent in the New Economy

A CAUTIONARY TALE OF TWO AGENTS

You've read Chapter 5, and you've acquired all the right tools to do business in the modern environment. So, you have your tools, you know what the customer wants, and you are the ruler of the Internet. Now you're set for success in the new economy, right? Well, maybe. There's an old joke about economists: When they see something work in reality, they wonder if it will work in theory. The point is that knowledge and application are two different things, and one does not assume the other. They can be extremes, and you can find agents on both ends.

Let's call the two extremes Cyber Agent and Old Pro. Cyber Agent has a Web site that attracts customers. The site is loaded; on it, she provides useful information for the consumer, advising him about buying and selling houses, linking him to neighborhood sites that describe the environment in which he may wish to live, and describing all the homes for sale in those neighborhoods using visual home tours. She has provided an e-mail link to contact her in case he wants to enter the market, along with links to mortgage and title companies to help smooth the transition to ownership. She checks e-mail at least three times a day and responds promptly to client and customer requests.

On her laptop, she has templates for listing presentations that are active, colorful, and attractive. It has a wireless modem that allows her to download the latest listings from the MLS and whisk them off to interested customers electronically. The laptop—which has a docking station to allow her to work at the office and at home as well on the move—contains all the forms necessary to complete a transaction. The forms are set up so that any piece of information (property location, buyer's identity, seller's identity, etc.) needs to be entered only once and then can be sent to any part of the form that requires it.

Cyber Agent has completed transactions both locally and across great distances, even internationally, in record time and with maximum efficiency, without ever having met in person the principals to the transaction. This is a good thing, because Cyber Agent is not good with people. She is awkward and ill at ease in crowds, and she feels more at home with technology than with customers. Cyber Agent is young, and to her this is not an unacceptable or even unusual state of affairs. After all, she deals with most of her friends electronically, through phone calls and e-mails and instant messaging. Why shouldn't business be any different?

Enter Old Pro. Old Pro has been in the business for 25 years, has been successful, and knows what works with people. The key to the business for Old Pro is networking. He belongs to the country club, attends Rotary faithfully, and lunches regularly with mortgage bankers, title insurers, and attorneys. He knows that the more involved he becomes in the business community in his market area, the more referrals will come his way. Even if this were not so, Old Pro would still be active in local affairs, because he's a baby boomer and that's what boomers do.

To keep up with his peers, he is active in the local real estate association. In the process, he even served a term as president. This not only kept him prominently in the minds of the local brokers and agents, it also allowed him to go to national meetings where he met REALTORS® from other parts of the country, which in turn led to long-distance referrals. All of these networking efforts have created a book of business that has been very profitable in the past.

Old Pro doesn't use much in the way of tools. He's got a cell phone, but doesn't everyone? The number isn't on his business card, by the way. His broker got him e-mail, but he doesn't use it much, checking it maybe once every three days or so. His calendar is paper, and his listing presentations are some printed materials that stress his experience and his success and contain some testimonials from past customers. In short, he's very low tech. Yet, he is very well organized with an eye to detail. Nothing falls through the cracks with Old Pro, even though he has to work 60 hours a week.

Put Old Pro in front of people and the deal is done. He is charming, empathetic, smooth, and convincing. He knows when to talk terms and when to ask for the sale. His sellers have never left any money on the table, and his buyers are carefully tended. After the transaction, both groups speak well of him and his repeat business rate is really good, despite the fact that his after-sale care consists of an annual calendar and a postcard every few months.

IN THE MERRY OLD LAND OF OZ

No one is either Cyber Agent *or* Old Pro.[1] Every successful agent is a mix of the two, adopting new technology as it can help business, yet remaining sensitive to the needs and moods of the market and its consumers. That's a good thing, because neither Cyber Agent nor Old Pro will win in the new economy.

There's a scene in the *Wizard of Oz* when Dorothy and her companions enter the presence of the great and powerful Oz. Thunder rolls, smoke billows, and the voice of the wizard booms out as his fierce image materializes on the curtain. All this, of course, inspires awe in the observers, until Toto crawls under the curtain. It is then revealed that a little old man behind the curtain controls all the pyrotechnics in the hall. When the secret is out, he turns out to be a charming old gent who just happens to make the wishes of the Scarecrow, the Tin Man, the Cowardly Lion, and even Dorothy come true.

The winning agent in the new economy has to be the reverse of the Wizard of Oz. In front of the curtain is the kindly, people-

---

[1] Who, by the way, have never met. They both work for a savvy manager who understands that old-timers can easily convince newcomers who bubble with technological knowhow that the new ways can never work and that they need to adopt the traditional way of doing things.

friendly, helpful agent; behind it is powerful, modern technological machinery that allows dreams to come true. This is different from the way it was in the old economy. Every agent has dealt with scarecrows and tin men and cowardly lions as clients and customers. Making their dreams come true in the past was merely a matter of producing a diploma or a clock or a medal. Now, there has to be just as much care, but more substance and infinitely better connectivity. You need both to get the job done.

PARTNERSHIP AND DELEGATION

Being both Cyber Agent and Old Pro is the ideal, but it's not always possible for the typical agent. Rather, you will shade your practice one way or the other and be better at one aspect than at the other.[2] That's OK, because your best interests lie in concentrating on what you do best and filling in the rest. That should not stand in the way of achieving the ideal as long as you use all the resources at your disposal. What are these?

- *The resources of the company.* Larger companies will have their own technological staff dedicated to creating the cocoon that every agent needs in the new economy. As we saw in Chapter 6, one of the major models for the broker is "servicing the agent," in which the broker creates the technology necessary for the agent to succeed and then makes it available. Every franchise and every major company operates to some degree under this model. If you are more Old Pro than Cyber Agent (and this covers the majority of REALTORS®), these resources are invaluable to you in becoming the complete new-economy agent. Find them and use them. If you need to understand them better, get close to the technologists at your company; they will be glad to tutor you.

-----

[2] Most agents will be more Old Pro than Cyber Agent, simply because they have been in the business longer and are used to doing business on a more personal basis. This is a good thing, because it's easier to find the technological resources to support Old Pro than it is to give a personality transplant to Cyber Agent.

- *The resources of the real estate community.* Top producers have created a model that is very useful to the agent seeking to succeed in the new economy. They have created teams that are, in effect, companies within companies. Each of the team members executes a specific function: farming, customer relations, transaction management, etc. This has two benefits. First, it allows each team member to specialize in a particular part of the process. That will increase productivity and efficiency (a principle that goes back to the granddaddy of all economists, Adam Smith, in the 18th century). Second, and perhaps more important, it frees agents to do what they do best—listing, selling, and cultivating clients and customers.

- *The resources of the wider community.* In Chapter 4, we read about the core competencies for the new real estate business and mentioned marketing through the effective use of information. That can be done only with the help of database professionals. Similarly, if you need to become Cyber Agent but lack the resources within your own company to do so, tapping the resources of the community in which you do business is a solution. At any college or university, there are faculty members and graduate students who can identify the tools you need, find them, and explain to you how they work. In effect, these resources act in the place of those provided by large companies for their agents.

The key here is that the new economy has made the real estate business very complicated. Achieving success requires not only more work but also more skill. There are ways of acquiring those skills on your own, and we discuss these in the next section. However, the shortest path to creating the kind of business that will succeed in the new environment is to cooperate with the resources that already exist. The "buy, not build" approach rests on partnering and delegating. *Partnership* entails cooperating with other real estate professionals and with those outside the industry to create the total package. *Delegating* means splitting up the tasks associated with the real estate transaction and assigning pieces to specialists, thus freeing your own time to do what you do best.

LIFELONG LEARNING

Neither delegation nor partnership precludes your need to participate in lifelong learning. This is not what you think it is. For most real estate professionals, "lifelong learning" is associated with either continuing education or designation education. Continuing education in the majority of cases is a farce. It is merely a requirement that you sit in a given spot for a given number of hours and expose yourself to a curriculum approved by a state commission. There is no pattern to the courses in the sense that they add up to a set of useful skills, nor is there any method to ensure that learning has taken place. If you wish to read or nap or pay bills during the continuing education course, that is just as worthy as if you took copious notes, followed up on all reading the instructor recommended and became a better practitioner. Yet, everyone who attended the session receives the same certification.[3] It is the equivalent of the scarecrow's diploma.

Designation courses are better because they address practical skills that the real estate professional needs in the execution of the business. Or at least those that were needed in the old economy. For the most part, they have not been updated to reflect the new economy, the added complexities of the real estate business, or the new technology of real estate.

The lifelong-learning experience requires that you absorb skills that will help you present a more attractive value proposition to the consumer. Some of this will increase your personal knowledge and skills, and some will enable you to manage your practice better. Two examples will suffice:

- *Managing your practice.* Most managers of real estate offices are salespeople who have been promoted. They have had very little in the way of management training and thus are ill prepared to become channels of company goals and policy (as middle managers should be.) Their performance would be improved by the application of accounting, personnel management, and communications courses available at the

---

[3] There is some hope for continuing education in that distance-learning channels are now available and facilitate examination of understanding. The curricula, however, still lag behind the needs of the industry.

local community college. Similarly, agents need these skills in managing their own practices. In addition, the training will allow the more effective creation of a team and the delegation of specific responsibilities within that team.

- *Increasing your skills.* Supra has recently developed a device that marries the Palm organizer with an electronic lockbox. The device can also be combined with a wireless modem to allow for access to MLS data, e-mail, and client information. It is a handy, all-in-one device that allows the real estate professional to provide instantaneous customer service and thus a more attractive value proposition. But managing this piece of personal technology will require initiative to get the training necessary. More than that, because this device will be superseded by other, more sophisticated ones, it requires a commitment to search out and master any device that will allow for increased consumer service.[4]

Commitment to continuous improvement means more than the accumulation of pieces of paper. The proof of lifelong learning is not on the wall of your office or den; it's in the service you provide to the clients and customer with whom you deal.

REMAKING THE AGENT MODEL: THE CONSUMER RULES

The emphasis we continually place on the consumer is not overdone. One of the basics of the new economy is the individual empowerment it generates. This means that nothing will happen in the new economy unless the consumer wants it to happen. Your success will be based on the creation of a compelling value proposition in the marketplace. Short of being the best option for the consumer, you have no other path to success.

While the blending of technology with personal service is the formula for success in the new economy, given the power of

---

[4] Fidelity National Information Solutions (FNIS) has a mobile product for MLS and transaction information.

the consumer in the marketplace, the blend will work only if done in the context of the way the new consumer approaches the market. As we discussed in Chapter 4, the consumer's value proposition is all about time and stress. To the degree that you can give the consumer time by expediting the transaction and to the degree that you can reduce stress by streamlining the transaction, you create consumer value. Your ability to leverage both your own personal expertise and technology will determine how much time and stress value you create.

NEW MODELS OF COMPENSATION

But that's only one part of the equation. The other side is the cost the consumer must pay for the value created. Traditionally, that has meant six percent of the sales price of the property for the seller, with the buyer paying whatever part of that the market would allow to be built into the price. More recently, with the advent of buyer's agency, the buyer has paid an explicit price for distinct representation in the transaction. Discount brokers have offered lesser sets of services for lesser fees.

From time to time, consumers would question the size of the fees charged by REALTORS®, but with little effect. Now, the information provided by the Internet has made the questioning more insistent. Consumers understand that it takes as much effort to sell a high-priced house as a low-priced one, look at the dollar difference in commissions, and ask why.[5] Additionally, consumers can now do parts of the transaction—home search, mortgage application, appointments—by themselves on the Internet, leading to a desire to see reduced fees for reduced services. That option has not been available for the traditional real estate practitioner who offers one price for one set of services, no substitutions.

If real estate professionals are to create a compelling value proposition for the consumer, they must consider alternative

---

[5] This is especially true in a seller's market, as has been the rule in the housing market in the United States over the past five years. But the effect has merely been accelerated by the market, not caused by it. The pressure on compensation structure and level will continue even as the market slows.

pricing systems. They must balance the time- and stress-reduction offerings with a cost structure that makes them worth buying on the part of the consumer. There are two basic approaches to doing this.

1. *Fee for service.* One of the major effects of the new information technology on the real estate business is the ability to break the process of the transaction, from first encounter to final closing, into discrete parts. Thus, property search leads to mortgage application and contract negotiation. After the contract has been accepted, the title needs to be cleared, the home appraised and inspected, the mortgage approved, and the closing established. Finally, all the papers need to be signed, the checks exchanged, and the deed change recorded. For each of these tasks, there are two principals, buyer and seller, but many possible agents (including the principals). Additionally, each of these takes a calculable amount of time.

    The fee-for-service approach allows the consumer to choose which of these services to purchase from the real estate professional, based on a posted rate. That rate, in turn, is based on an hourly rate established by the real estate professional. The total cost to the consumer is then the sum of all the services purchased and the relevant costs attached.

2. *Real estate consultancy.* The second option is priced the same as the first but differs because the relationship between consumer and real estate professional is a consultative one rather than an agency relationship.[6] The consultant is an expert in all aspects of the real estate market and is ready to advise the consumer as to the best way to accomplish all the tasks in the real estate process. In theory, the prices charged by the real estate consultant will be less than the fees for service charged by the agent because the agency liability is missing; thus, overhead is lower with the consultant.

---

[6] For a full exposition of this approach, see Julie Garton-Good, *Real Estate a la Carte: Selecting the Services You Need, Paying What They're Worth,* Chicago, Dearborn, 2001.

The fee-for-service approach is appealing in a market where consumers rule. It maximizes their choices and aligns the real estate industry with other businesses whose charges are based on work performed, not tied to the value of the object being serviced.[7]

IMPLEMENTING THE NEW MODEL

But how do you calculate your fees? The answer to this goes back to the point made above about the need for some business training in order to manage your practice. Most real estate professionals have no knowledge of how to calculate their costs. If you ask an agent how much it costs to get a listing, she would probably not know where to start. In calculating a fee structure, you need to start with the basic costs of your business, including your own compensation, and then project them across the number of hours you will work.

In calculating the basic cost of your business, consider the following elements:

- *Transportation:* How much does it cost you to operate and maintain your vehicle for use in your business? Take the total annual cost of the vehicle and multiply by the percentage of time or distance required by work. Thus, if it costs you $14,000 a year to operate and maintain a vehicle that is used for work 50 percent of the time, this figure is $7,000.
- *Professional services:* How much do you pay your broker and outside vendors for office space, telephone, advertising, personal marketing, etc.? These are direct business costs and make up a good part of your business overhead.
- *Technology:* How much does it cost you to maintain the technology you use in your business? This includes cell phone costs, laptop and other devices, and the training that accompanies them. If you acquire a computer or some

---

[7] Imagine going to a mechanic to have your car serviced and being quoted a price equal to a percentage of the car's value. It would seem strange, to say the least.

other tool in a given year, figure how long you will use it and spread the cost over that period. Given the speed at which technology is progressing, two years is conservative, and expensing the tool in the year purchased is aggressive. Either is defensible.

- *Other costs:* These will include license and continuing education fees, REALTOR® organization dues, taxes, and any labor you hire as employees or contractors to help you run your practice.

Finally, add in *your own compensation.* There are two ways to do this. At one extreme, you can picture yourself as the Alex Rodriguez or the Madonna of real estate and put up a big number. Alternatively, you can look at what you might earn if you were not in real estate. In other words, what's your next best opportunity in the market? A safe middle ground might be to look at your tax returns for the last three years and average the taxable income numbers. Because the real estate business has been booming, this might be a bit more than the next few years may bring, but that's in your favor.

When you gather all these costs, your overhead, divide them by 2,080 (the number of hours in the work year).[8] The result is your hourly rate. For most REALTORS®, this number will be between $75 and $150 per hour. That corresponds roughly to the rate charged by most dentists and about half that of most attorneys.

You can then apply this rate in two different ways. The first is to charge your clients and customers an hourly rate and then provide an estimate of the time you will spend providing the agreed-on services for them. This estimate will serve as a reference point, with an agreement that the actual number cannot exceed 110 percent of that figure without the permission of the client. Most of us have dealt with this type of pricing when dealing with construction companies.

The second alternative is to prefigure the approximate time it takes to perform any of the discrete services you offer and then post a price for each service. Thus, if it takes eight hours to ne-

---

[8] Notice that this gives you a paid vacation and covers the costs that pile up, even when you're at the beach.

gotiate a contract and your hourly rate is $150, you would offer to negotiate a contract for $1,200. If it takes less time, you make money; if the negotiations drag out, you lose money. In general, because real estate transactions are so idiosyncratic, charging an hourly rate is probably more effective as an alternative compensation method to offer the public.

FINAL THOUGHTS

In the new economy, there will be increasing pressure on the traditional fee structure. Consumer power will force the real estate business to vary the way it offers services and charges for those services. Agents will likely be in the forefront of that change, and currently, the fee-for-service models are being implemented in many parts of the country by many agents.

But this method of pricing will not take over the industry and replace the commission system. As we pointed out in an earlier chapter, things in this life change slowly if they ever change at all. Rather, the fee-for-service model will become more prevalent over time and will join the commission system as a significant feature on the industry landscape. And it may well not be the only new entry.

It is probable that, ultimately, pricing in the real estate industry will come to resemble the legal business. Attorneys charge contingency fees (usually in civil cases), just as REALTORS® now charge commissions. But they also charge on a fee-for-service basis. If you go to an attorney to draw up a will, a trust agreement, or a prenuptial pact, you will be charged a set fee, based on the attorney's work input. No attorney will charge a percentage of the estate value to draw up a will. So, too, REALTORS® will charge for their services on a fee basis, calculated as above. Finally, attorneys offer retainer relationships. While this is a bit far-fetched now, it is conceivable that some real estate agent will make this sort of arrangement work in the real estate industry.

Chapter 8

New Models for Associations

The ultimate role of the REALTOR® organization is to help shape and influence a favorable business environment for its members. Each REALTOR® association has the responsibility to efficiently and effectively provide value to its members. While the operating framework in which an association chooses to serve its members may vary depending on its organizational structure, demographics, size, available resources and diversity of needs, there are many creative ways to deliver and optimize value, even with limited resources.[1]

Changes in the economy and changes in the way information flows to business have altered the services that individuals and firms seek from their trade associations. This is especially true in the real estate industry, where sensitivity to regulation and to individual membership combine to place unique pressures on associations. In a sense, associations are no different from other businesses in the new economy. Both face the same pressures in providing customer service and value.

---

[1] AEC Association Models Work Group, National Association of REALTORS®, "REALTOR® Association Models," June 27, 2001.

There are two differences that set associations apart from other businesses. First, for associations, their owners, their customers, and their work force are all the same people. This places additional demands on customer service that simply are not present in the for-profit sector. Second, members who determine association programs, policies, and services often act on their motivations as businesspeople rather than association fiduciaries. This is especially true in organizations such as real estate associations, where the membership is composed of individuals and small-business owners.

This chapter traces the changes that have occurred in the environment facing associations and how those changes have altered the way in which real estate associations serve their members. Understanding the new services that are required and needed by their members is crucial to the success and survival of associations in the new economy.

CHANGES IN THE ENVIRONMENT FACING REAL ESTATE ASSOCIATIONS

To be successful in the new economy, any business needs to understand and anticipate the needs of its customers. For real estate associations, this means understanding the needs of members who are facing changes in their own business climate. We discussed some of the broader trends in Chapter 2. For associations, the implications of these trends fall into three general categories: demographic and social, economic, and technological. What are the specific trends most likely to shape the association business during the near future, say, in the next five to ten years?

Demographics

The dominant force of the latter part of the twentieth century was the baby boom. Boomers created American history in all of its highs, lows, ups, and downs. They were responsible for the growth of the 1950s, the turmoil of the 1960s, the stagnation of the 1970s and the booms of the 1980s and 1990s. Because the ethic of the baby boomers strongly emphasizes participation, as-sociations benefited from this dominance through an abundance of highly talented individuals who volunteered for association work.

Now that generation is aging, and its members' enthusiasm for volunteer work is waning. Associations are increasingly chal-lenged to generate the level of participation they have come to rely on and on which they have built their programs. More im-portantly, the generations following the baby boom don't share the same ethic. The surest way to get baby boomers to do any-thing was to use the magic phrase, "You can make a difference." That doesn't work with Gen-Xers, who are more interested in in-stant gratification and lack the persistence it takes to stick with an association workload.

The second major demographic feature that marks the new century is the significant flow of immigrants who have entered the United States. This cuts two ways. First, immigrants are avid for home ownership as their piece of the American dream, but they view the real estate market in the context of their own cul-tural norms. Real estate association members need to be aware of the cultural training they need to service this new customer base.

Second, newcomers to the United States will increasingly enter the real estate business. Ideally, traditional real estate asso-ciations would welcome their membership by using a number of languages beside English to communicate with newcomers and reach out to include them in the associations' operations. Unfortunately, this challenge remains largely unanswered, and traditional associations remain as homogeneous now as they have been in the past. At the same time, specialty associations, formed around national group or common language, have evolved to fill the gap.

Economy and Society

For most Americans, time has become the scarcest natural resource. For the consumer, value has become measured in terms of time saved and stress reduced. Associations face a simi-lar market in *their* customers, that is, their members. Members increasingly value time and will work within associations only if it can fit the time pressures of their lives.

This is a challenge for associations. They have always served a networking function and have designed their programs to take as much time as possible to allow for active members to get to know each other and forge strong personal bonds. In that sense, associations are less like businesses and more like congregations. So associations create numbers of standing committees with regular meetings and extended work schedules. This structure has increasingly less appeal in a more frantic, time-compressed environment. Given the changing of the guard from boomers to Gen-Xers, this challenge is even more significant and difficult.

The marketplace for associations has also become more competitive. Besides ethnic associations, groups focusing on particular issues and particular subspecialties of real estate have also entered the scene. Associations have become subject to a phenomenon termed "transactional membership," meaning that members will give their loyalty to those associations that create for them the greatest value in furthering the members' businesses. So, if the association charges $100 in annual dues and delivers (in the eyes of the member) $99 in value, then the bond between member and organization is tenuous. Reverse those numbers and the bond will be almost unbreakable.

The challenge here is to create a compelling value proposition for the member. This, of course, mirrors the new economy's pressures on real estate practitioners to create value for their customers. In the past, both businesses were automatic: The REALTOR® was the only game in town and the REALTOR® association was the only option for association services. Both models have disappeared. In their place, there is the need to prove your worth to your constituents every time you interact with them.

Technology

Once again, the changes that have affected the way in which we treat and transmit information present challenges for associations. First, the close connection between real estate associations and MLSs becomes significantly harder to manage in the technological environment. The pressure on the MLS to increase its technological sophistication and product mix will push it to make business technology more complex and (at least initially) more expensive for the real estate practitioner. This coincides with the goal of the association to make life easier for its members. Increasingly, the conflicts between these two competing ends will force associations to rethink their involvement with MLSs at the risk of depriving their members of the tools they need for success in the new economy.

Second, real estate practitioners, particularly smaller operatives, will look to the association for information about the technology they need for success. For larger associations, this is not a problem, as most will have a technology specialist on staff who can serve that function.[2] For smaller associations, however, the inability to serve as the information source will reduce the value that members think they receive from the association. Even if the association can serve as the information source for technology, there is an added challenge involved with technological change. As we have seen in Chapter 6, many if not all of the large real estate firms—franchises and independents—have developed their own tools that they would like their associates to use. Often these are proprietary, and the training associated with their use is also conducted by the firm. They see it as part of their competitive edge. The association that provides technology information equally to all its members may be seen by the larger firms as competing directly against them, using dollars provided from their associates' dues.

Finally, associations need to create their own technological operation to communicate with their members and provide them with the information the association develops. This requires resources. In the current environment, where most real estate associations are static in membership, this poses a dilemma: The resources for technology must be generated either by increasing dues or by redirecting funds from other projects. The former is politically difficult and takes a great deal of time, while the latter runs the risk of sacrificing the pet activity of a

---

[2] A particularly good example of how this happens can be found in *Real Estate Technology,* the excellent magazine published by the California Association of REALTORS®.

long-time active member and damaging the association's role as a congregation.

There are many different challenges facing associations in the new economy, but they can generally be grouped as how to find ways to

- energize and attract members though a clear value proposition;
- increase the recognition of the association in its various communities;
- allocate resources efficiently;
- optimize competitive position.

If an association can successfully address these challenges, it will be successful in the new economy. What models can be used to address them?

REALTOR® ASSOCIATION MODELS

There are a variety of models that can be adopted by REALTOR® associations. Traditionally, these associations have operated in ways that provide advocacy for issues of concern to the membership and create business and personal networking opportunities for the members. Therefore, a large percentage of the association's resources are devoted to political, legislative, regulatory, and public affairs, and regular meetings dot the calendar.

The operating styles of these associations range across a fairly wide spectrum. At one end of the spectrum (generally populated by smaller associations), members run the organization and paid staff carry out the orders of volunteer leadership. At the other end, larger associations tend to place more responsibility for operations on staff, with members setting policy and letting paid staff execute.

NAR describes this spectrum in three models for associations: administrative, management, and leadership.[3]

---

[3] Association Models Work Group, op. cit.

1. *Administrative level:* Member-focused, knows basic activities of its REALTOR® constituencies, and knows where to find information that is important to members in conducting their daily business activities. This model is foundational. It represents the minimum competency/ service level a REALTOR® organization may offer. In such an association, staff will possess a general familiarity in legal, regulatory, and business issues, relying on significant volunteer involvement and working relationships with other service organizations.

2. *Management level:* A credible source of information, proficient in identifying and proactively communicating business practices and trends that affect the association's member constituencies. This is a second-level model and represents the advanced competency/service level that a REALTOR® organization may offer. In such associations, the staff will possess a proficiency in managing and communicating legal, regulatory, and business issues affecting the association and will effectively manage association business, relying on volunteer involvement and working relationships with other service organizations.

3. *Leadership level:* Initiates policy formation and advocacy on all levels and seeks and implements innovative and creative programs, products, and services that ultimately provide enhanced value for all REALTOR® association constituencies. The model presumes a high level of sophistication, innovation, and proactivity. It represents the highest competency/service level that a REALTOR® organization may offer. In such associations the staff will possess expertise and provide leadership in legal, regulatory, and business issues that affect the association and will transparently manage association business. At this level the association relies on volunteer input and strategic partnerships and offers working relationships with other service organizations.

While these models can serve as a basic guideline for how real estate associations are organized, the challenges of the new economy and the changes affecting associations require another kind of model, one that describes how the real estate association can create a compelling value proposition for its members. This model focuses on creating an association that is *fast, fluid, and flexible*. In this context, *fast* refers to the quality of an association that can understand and respond to member needs and concerns in a way that each member regards as exceeding expectations. *Fluid* refers to the association's ability to engage members in a clear vision and to make decisions in an effective manner. *Flexible* means that an association has the ability to form and re-form itself to achieve a specified set of end results that further the vision and create value for the members.

AN ASSOCIATION MUST BE FAST

Information empowers the consumer and levels the market. But information is also a tool that the providers of goods and services need to succeed in the new economy. If an association is to provide a compelling value proposition for its members, it needs to know what the members would include in that value proposition. That involves having an intimate knowledge of the members' businesses, the challenges they face, and the help the association can provide.

For an association to be fast, it needs to do three things.

1. Find Out What the Members Think

Most associations conduct surveys of their membership in some form. Most ask sales-related questions; few ask marketing questions. The difference is simple: Selling involves getting people to buy what you have, while marketing seeks to find out what people want and then create it for them. The typical association survey asks members to rate existing services and products without asking whether these are the products and services the members feel they need from the association. One of the best surveys I ever received came from my trade association, the American Society of Association Executives. It asked about my expectations for service from the association. How many rings before the telephone is answered? How much time should elapse before staff answers a letter (fax, e-mail)? In other words, it wanted to know what I wanted from the association. It didn't try to sell me on products it happened to have or enlist me to serve on some committee.

The fast association will take the time to know and appreciate its members' businesses and use this information to guide the creation of association offerings. The fast association will field at least one mail survey per year and conduct focus groups of its members at annual meetings. Part of these inquiries ought to be devoted to how the member likes to receive information. In this electronic society, it is easy to customize delivery systems to meet the members' wishes. This information allows for a systematic flow of input to and from members and allows the association to be responsive to members' concerns and needs.

2. Touch the Members at Every Opportunity

Most associations (in all industries) regularly touch only a top layer of members. These are the actives that man the committees, show up at annual meetings, and have personal contact with staff on a regular basis. The vast majority of the membership is never personally touched. Recently, a real estate association conducted focus groups of its nonactive members to learn what they thought of the association's services. It turned out that these services had to be listed for the members before they could respond; they had little to no idea what they were. So surveys and focus groups are not going to provide much additional member contact, especially when held at the annual meetings that the regulars attend anyway. Rather, the association must take every opportunity to touch every member it can.

In smaller associations, this is not as hard as it sounds. Most local associations have a board of directors of between 15 and 20 people. If each director can meet once a month with a group of members, the association within a year can touch virtually every member. If each director met with 25 members a month, doable with the size of most real estate firms, 15 board members could meet with up to 4,500 members in a year. That covers the vast majority of local (and most state) associations.[4]

---

[4] In larger organizations, going to the membership may take other forms. In May 2001, the leadership and key staff of the Florida Association of REALTORS® undertook a six-day "caravan" to six different parts of the state to bring information to the membership and to understand their concerns. This brought out large crowds and allowed a hands-on association experience.

These contacts with members increase the sensitivity of the association to its customers and allow for a better sense of the market in which it operates. This can be augmented by asking members specific questions about issues of current concern contained in dues billing letters, in monthly newsletters, and in any other communication between the association and the membership. Of course, none of this serves its purpose unless it is shared, discussed, and integrated into the decision-making process of the association. We discuss how that is done later.

3. Focus on customer service

The ultimate in consumer value for any business in the new economy is customer service. We have evolved as an economy from selling goods and services to providing an experience for the customer. The fast association will create that experience both by understanding the needs and wants of the membership and by satisfying them through the channels with which the customer is most comfortable, but also by being responsive in dealing with members' contacts and requests. In an age when communication is instantaneous, the operations of the association must be focused on matching the speed and accuracy of the best in the business world.

This means investing in technology. The communications systems used by the association are its lifeline with its members. These need to be of the highest quality available so that each individual member feels that he or she is the only customer the association has. That means being able to instantly access the full record of every member's contacts with the association (education courses taken, products bought, meetings attended, etc.) so that any staff talking with any member can exhibit a friendly familiarity.

AN ASSOCIATION MUST BE FLUID

Fluidity, in the context of association business, means the ability to create a vision that will excite members and to use information in its decision-making processes. First, the vision must be clear and point at a future state that reflects where the members want the association to be. Consider the following vision:

> **Our core purpose is to encourage, facilitate, and recognize the highest standards of professionalism in the practice of real estate and to ensure that our members remain vital to the transfer of real property. We are recognized as the ultimate expert and source of information about real estate–related issues and topics by legislators, members, the business community, and customers.**

Many real estate associations could espouse this vision. The vision consists of two parts, the core ideology and the envisioned future. The core purpose (the organization's reason for being—the idealistic motivation for doing the organization's work)—here the first sentence—focuses directly on the relationship of the association and its members. The envisioned future[5] paints a picture of the association as it relates to the various publics it serves. It places the association in a key role with respect to those publics and offers a value proposition to them.

Visions are small-group products. They are developed through a strategic thinking process that ought to involve only the key volunteer and staff leadership of the association. This in itself might be a departure from standard operating practice of associations in which "planning" is done by a large group developed to touch all political bases within the association.[6]

The second hallmark of fluidity is the manner in which associations make decisions. Traditionally, associations make decisions based on who is in the room. Political bases must be touched, and the key active members must be included in the process. Often the result is a decision based on conventional wis-

---

[5] The envisioned future of any association is the world that it wishes to create as a result of its actions. The future centers around a Big Audacious Goal (BAG) that can be accomplished in 15 or 20 years, the pursuit of which will bring the association closer to its desired future position.

[6] If this planning is done in a crisis, it would be well to remember the thinking of Einstein who commented that no problem was ever solved by the consciousness that created it.

dom ("We've always done it that way"), prior precedent ("We tried that once and it didn't work"), or assumed information ("The members would want us to do that.") None of these methods will lead to success in the new economy. They may preserve the "club" but not serve the end goals of the association.

Decision making should be based on the use of all the information that bears upon the question under consideration.[7] This is the use for all the information gathered by the "fast" association. Essentially the information is sorted into four categories:

1. What information do we have that pertains to the question? Have we both gathered and shared all we can know about it? How would alternative solutions affect the path toward our long-term vision?
2. What resources does the association possess that would enable the treatment of this question? Given our financial health and human capabilities, can we tackle the issue?
3. What is the strategic position of the association in this issue? Are we best positioned to handle the question, or can the answer be best found in another organization?
4. How does this question relate to values and the ethics espoused by the association?

Answering each of these questions will lead the association to a good answer to the question under review. The answer may not work, but it will be a good answer, one within the capacity of the association and in support of its vision.

In establishing the answers to these questions, the association will pass through two stages. The first stage is *dialogue,* which is aimed at airing all the information, developing options, and discussing the implications of each option. In dialogue, no positions are taken and no options argued. The result of the process will be a full development of all dimensions of the decision and all po-

---

[7] The system described here is called "knowledge-based" governance. A knowledge-based organization is a *transactional enterprise.* The primary currency of those transactions is information and insight. Who makes the decision is far less important than the quality of information and insight on which the decision is made. It is best outlined in Glenn Tecker, Kermit Eide, and Jean Frankel, *Knowledge-based Decision Making,* ASAE Foundation, 1999.

tential options. The second part of the process is *deliberation,* which is designed to reach a decision. Now the traditional advocacy process with which we are all familiar takes place. There are two differences between this process and the usual decision-making practices of the association. First, the basis of the decision is information and knowledge about the issue and the association. Second, dialogue is added to deliberation to enable the full exposition of all that is known about the issue.

THE ASSOCIATION MUST BE FLEXIBLE

The intensive collection and use of information to understand members and to lead to decision making must lead to effective implementation. That requires that the association be flexible in its structures and processes. As a general rule, the creation of vision and the development of strategic direction are responsibilities of the volunteer leadership but are usually done with participation by staff. Implementation, however, is the responsibility of staff, with oversight by member volunteers.

That oversight will flow through the board of directors, and it implies a change in the way the board operates to create flexibility. As its essence, the board of directors specifies end results, allocates resources, and then inspects whether the results have been accomplished. It creates work groups, consisting of members and staff, around desired end results. These work groups are charged with the accomplishment of specific objectives and are led by, and consist of, the most qualified individuals, whether members, staff, or outside experts. Each ceases to exist when it has accomplished its task.[8] While they are in existence, staff and volunteer work groups will report only when they confront obstacles with which the board has to deal. Contrast this with the traditional creation of standing committees, filled by political necessity, that report at every opportunity (whether or not there is anything of substance to report) and exist in perpetuity, regardless of the needs of the association.

---

[8] Associations will still need some standing committees, but these will be small in number and confined to those mandated in the bylaws as key to the existence of the organization.

With the board's role in implementation limited, its activities must then be focused on discussing and planning the future of the association. The board of a flexible association will spend the majority of its time using information: A portion of each meeting should be devoted to presenting and discussing what is known about the members' needs and desires. Ideally, this will be information provided by the staff and the volunteer leadership that touches the membership. Issues of capacity, core capability, and strategic position will be routinely considered in deciding how to provide a value proposition to the members. In other words, the vast majority of board time will be focused on issues of strategic direction and policy.

To do all this, the board needs to carefully screen what items should go on the agenda and what should not, and adopt meeting processes that facilitate the board's movement from dialogue to deliberation:

- Reports should be placed on the consent agenda, to be brought up and discussed only if a director feels strongly enough to do so.
- A director should be charged with the responsibility to monitor the relevance of the board's discussion to the association's plan and its adherence to the rules of dialogue and deliberation.
- Discussions should be held at each meeting about the external environment and how it is affecting the business of the members.

Put another way, the board of directors of the flexible association will function as corporate overseer, hiring the chief staff executive and ensuring that end results are achieved. It will operate as a policy maker, crafting positions on topics of concern to the members in a way that facilitates the pursuit of the vision. It will also operate as a panel of judges, deliberating issues using full information, choosing among potential options, and deciding issues of dispute presented by work groups.

RESPONDING TO THE NEW ECONOMY

It is likely impossible that real estate associations will survive in the new economy without changing to accommodate the pressures it places on them. The number of associations has already shrunk significantly and continues to do so. The reason is basic: The new economy ignores geography, and real estate associations are essentially geographic entities. Their market areas are delineated down to the street or county line. The reality of the new economy is that these boundaries have no real meaning anymore. Hence, we have seen cross-border mergers, such as the Greater Capital Area Association of REALTORS® in the Washington, D.C. area, that recognize the reality of market.

The only organizing principle that makes sense for the real estate association is the delivery of value to a member base. If it cannot do this, transactional membership dictates that the association will disappear. Creating value means recognizing how the new economy affects members and potential members and understanding how the association can contribute to the success of its constituents.

Change is hard, and there are enough long-term active members around to make it harder. The key to making the changes necessary to survive lies with a strong and committed leadership. Vision is the beginning, and vision is a top-down process because leadership is the art of creating and enrolling followers in a compelling vision. The second step is the implementation of the vision through a revised association decision-making structure that is based on knowledge about the needs and wants of the members and the environment in which the association will operate.

The model contained in this chapter is highly stylized, which means that its application will differ given individual association environments, sizes, culture, and location. But it does contain the elements that will allow the association to adapt to the new economy and be successful.

Chapter 9

Is There a Role
for the MLS?

No part of the real estate industry has been as shaken by technology as the multiple-listing service (MLS). Historically, MLSs have had dual business purposes. They were primarily information repositories, taking listings from brokers and agents and formatting them for use in the transaction flow. As restricted access information banks, they were the bedrock of the old real estate business model, in which the public dealt with, and was willing to pay, real estate professionals because they alone—thanks to the MLS—had the full overview of the real estate market.

The emergence of the Internet and the growth of companies such as Homestore and HomeAdvisor.com and the subsequent emergence of broker web sites have eroded the information function of the MLS. In addition, the advent of broker reciprocity has spread the information formerly held by MLSs to frequently visited public Web sites. The result is that MLSs are now only one among many choices for information by both real estate professionals and the public, and their presentation is stodgy relative to the Internet. In short, if MLSs consider themselves in the information business, they will soon be extinct. They need a new business model.

But MLSs are also communications systems, linking agents and brokers from different firms into a system that can accomplish transactions. That aspect of the system is regularly used by member practitioners and is the most effective method yet devised for making real estate transactions happen smoothly. That familiarity suggests a concentration on the communications side of the business as a survival strategy. But the complexity of technology has made this difficult for the MLS to accomplish. There are, however, a number of strategies that can create the new business for the new economy that will allow MLSs to prosper. This chapter develops those strategies and strings them together into a new model for the MLS.[1]

THE PROBABLE FUTURE FOR THE MLS BUSINESS

Any business model that works for the MLS business must recognize the most probable future environment in which MLSs will operate. You can never predict the future. But given what we know about change in the real estate industry and what we know about the evolution of technology, we can make some reasonably satisfying guesses. Here are the main elements of the MLS future along with their implications for MLSs if they are accurate:

- *Cross-boundary cooperation.* MLSs across the country will be linked and operate together to provide information to all members. Over the past decade, we have seen the emergence of regional MLSs that cross state boundaries in the Philadelphia and Washington, D.C., areas and of metropolitan regionals in Seattle, Denver, Milwaukee, and Chicago. These MLSs have been able to serve as unifying points for the real estate business in those markets. Now the major regional MLSs are in conversations about some sort of cooperative arrangements that would standardize their data platforms. The process of regionalization can only continue, particularly in light of the economies provided by information technology in the management and

---

[1] The material is based on the current plans and activities of a number of large regional MLSs. They cannot, of course, be specifically identified, nor can actual products, most of them in the planning stage, be named.

presentation of information. Ultimately, this linkage may possibly include a nationwide MLS, although that is unnecessary if standardization among MLSs is achieved.

• *The emergence of "niche" MLSs, systems that specialize in particular types of property or very specific geographic areas.* Conversely, the power of technology to create an information "vegematic," where the data are sliced and diced as one wishes, opens the door to smaller, more customized MLSs, serving more specific clientele and providing an information base that is richer and more detailed than is attainable for all practitioners in a given market. These specialized information sets are more likely to emerge in the higher-end market for property, where the payoff justifies the increased cost of creating a tool for a relatively small number of customers.

• *New types of technology that transcend the Internet and open up more efficient communication and transaction channels for the real estate practitioner.* The emergence of XML technology may be the biggest threat to the listing side of the broker and agent businesses and, by extension, to the MLS. XML is a programming language and standard that allows for any individual to place information on the Internet in a way that allows search engines to find that specific information. When this becomes standard for the Internet, each homeseller will become his or her own lister and each homebuyer his or her home agent. But XML also will have benefits for practitioners. By becoming experts in the placement of and search for real estate information, they can dramatically cut the time it takes to find a buyer or seller. It will also allow practitioners to bypass the MLS, further reducing its functionality as a provider of information.

• *New tools for the real estate practitioner in conjunction with these new channels.* In Chapter 5, we read about the tool kit the real estate professional will need to be current with the way of business in the new economy. Among these new tools are "e-platforms," for transactions and business management, and virtual services. There are currently no transaction-management systems that work, but there will be, and therein lies the implication for the MLS. As we shall see, it is entirely possible that the MLS will be the driving force to develop these systems and/or bring them into operational use within the industry. This requires that the MLS repurpose itself as a technology company.

- *Increased numbers of strategic alliances in the normal course of doing business as real estate practitioners attempt to expand value.* Any scan of the business news will demonstrate how important strategic relationships are in the new economy. The amount of competencies required to be successful and the number of opportunities in the marketplace almost compel businesses to seek partnerships. In fact, some of these partnerships will even include former competitors. It's the same way in real estate. To be successful in the new economy, real estate brokers and agents will need to form strategic alliances with other both inside and outside the industry. In the case of the MLS, this will be even truer. To remain relevant as a business system for the real estate industry, MLSs will forge alliances with technology companies, including other MLSs and system vendors such as Fidelity National Information Solutions (FNIS).

- *An end to proprietary data and therefore, a greater need to enhance and control data through a restructured MLS.* To the extent that MLSs can remain information (as opposed to communications) utilities, they must determine a way to create a much more detailed and augmented data set for real estate professionals. Simple provision of listing information does not create sufficient value to sustain subscriptions to the MLS. Information has value only if it is converted into knowledge, i.e., made actionable by the recipient.

THE NEW MODEL FOR THE MLS

To remain relevant to a rapidly improving and more sophisticated real estate industry, MLSs must shift their focus. They are facing competitive pressures not only from within the industry (as brokers and agents find new ways of managing the information they need to succeed) but also from the outside, as vendors increasingly find better ways to aggregate data and provide technological tools to the industry.[2]

To survive, MLSs must become, for their members, shareholders, and subscribers, the premier agencies for development and delivery of real estate information and technology services. At its heart, this means reconceiving MLSs as technology companies that provide not only information, but also essential data services to their members and that authenticate information by using widely accepted standards, provide leading-edge technology tools to real estate practitioners, and host the standard transaction platform for the real estate industry.

This is a tall order, but it can be approached at a number of different levels. Clearly, the degree of financial resources and technical expertise possessed by the MLS will determine how deeply it can go into the objectives listed above. In addition, market position will affect the ability of the MLS to establish a reputation as a technology company. It is probable that in the process of crafting a model that will allow for success in the new economy, MLSs will rely on strategic partnerships, particularly with larger MLSs. This, in turn, will result in the expansion of existing regional MLSs and the creation of new ones. So, like the industry it serves, the MLS business will continue to consolidate.

In the process of reaching the goal of being a technology company, MLSs will need to pay attention to certain strategies.

Develop Communications Mechanisms

How can an MLS become a valued component in the business success of members, shareholders and subscribers? Whatever development the MLS undertakes, it must be focused on the end user of the tools and services it provides. This process begins with communication with these end users to fully understand their needs with respect to the current system and any future enhancements. The best position for the MLS is to un-

---

[2] Interestingly, the savvier MLSs realize that this is the case. See the remarks of Jim Naccorato, president and CEO of the Wasatch Front Regional MLS (Utah and Idaho), on the relative technological positions of MLSs and outside aggregators (Rick Scher, "A Data-based Dilemma," *Inman News,* July 31, 2001).

derstand the needs of the end user before the end user does. This means creating an effective market-sensing mechanism (similar to that of associations, described in Chapter 8). This includes

- periodically surveying customers on user satisfaction. The surveys can be done formally or informally and need not be "scientifically correct." For example, the MLS can use the logon page in the system to solicit information/feedback from users.
- realizing that any direct feedback from stakeholder groups is good feedback.
- creating and/or expanding user groups as a member feedback tool. Marketing professionals have found that the best way to understand what customers think is to ask them. This strategy sounds simple but is rarely practiced.
- actively soliciting end-user advice on system enhancements. Software companies spend a great deal of money on beta testing. MLSs need to follow that lead, especially in the face of the competition they now see in the marketplace.

The corollary to this market-sensing communication is the creation and maintenance of clear channels for information to flow from the MLS to its stakeholders and back. Most MLSs are owned by real estate associations and are governed by a board of directors that represents these owners. Thus, the communications that pass between MLSs and their end users generally go through two intermediary steps.[3] I think we've all played the game of "telephone," so we know how messages become garbled as they are transmitted. Because of this possibility for misunderstandings, the creation and maintenance of a barrier-free communications system that links the MLS with its directors, shareholders, and end users is a key part of creating value and the perception of value.

I think you must begin by ensuring that the passage of information between the directors of the MLS and its shareholders

---

[3] There are exceptions. Technical interaction, as often happens through help desks, is direct from users and is thus extremely useful in understanding what members need and how the technology can best help them.

occurs in a timely and accurate manner. The board ought to understand clearly (from the point of director orientation) that when conducting MLS business, it is in neither the association business, the broker business, nor the agent business. The interests they are serving are the interests of the end user and the MLS, not those of the shareholder associations.

To ensure that those shareholders will also serve as an objective channel for communication between the MLS and the end users, the MLS needs to forge a strong, positive relationship with shareholder management and leadership. A double check on this process can be secured by developing direct communication links (through the MLS system or via e-mail) with end users, so that any snag in the flow of information can be bypassed. Ultimately, the end result the MLS needs in this relationship is the improvement of communications channels to the point where the MLS can distribute important, time-sensitive information to all end users and ensure that it reaches them.

Finally, you can improve the sizzle all you want, but you have to have the steak, too. Make sure that the performance of the system, its software, and the customer service operation meets and exceeds customer expectations. The consortium of large MLSs that is attempting to put together national standards for the MLS business is a marvelous opportunity in this regard. It will allow an MLS to benchmark with similarly sized MLS systems and allow for all MLSs to understand and manage to standards. It will also provide a context for MLSs to educate end users on standards.

Why all this is important can be illustrated with a story. Lamb is the fourth most popular meat in the United States (behind beef, chicken and pork, and maybe even turkey), and lamb producers face an uphill struggle for product recognition and acceptance. They attempted to help the cause with a massive publicity campaign to increase lamb consumption, targeting the Pacific Northwest. The response was terrific and consumers flocked (no pun intended) to the stores to buy lamb. Unfortunately, the supply of lamb had not been increased in the wake of the campaign, so consumers were frustrated by a lack of product. The campaign was a success, but the industry was worse off at the end than the beginning. Unless the MLS system is actually meeting the needs of the end users, no amount of communications or public relations will convince them that the MLS is their business partner.

Develop New Markets

To serve a broader customer base through geographic expansion, new markets must be developed. The economies of scale provided by information technology will inevitably drive consolidation in the MLS business. It's as easy to serve 40,000 users as it is to serve 10,000, spreading total costs over a larger base and driving down per-user price. In addition, scale allows for the introduction of new, advanced technologies on a cost-effective basis. The typical user gets a better system at a lower cost, and the advanced user can maximize performance. Thus, we will see the expansion of geographic areas served by MLSs in all markets. In a sense, this is merely an extension of the regionalization that has taken place over the past decade.

There is a second argument for geographic expansion as well. As technology makes the real estate market more efficient, there will be a gradual decline in the number of practitioners operating in the industry. For the MLS, this means a declining end-user base in any given geographic area. The long-term implications of this are higher prices for the end user and declining surplus growth for the MLS.

Saying why expansion makes sense is a lot easier than actually doing it, which is why I write books instead of running an MLS. Clearly, the first step is to adopt a long-range expansion plan. The first part of this process is the determination of the most likely areas into which to extend MLS services.[4] This is best done by integrating existing shareholders and end users into expansion planning. Any growth will directly affect them in terms of a change in their equity (shareholders) and a change in service levels (users). Bringing them in early is a useful tactic in accomplishing the end result.

---

[4] It's interesting to note that while the most likely expansion areas are probably physically adjacent to the MLS, technology allows the extension of information services to any area of the country.

Because expansion will entail absorbing the functions of another MLS, you will in all probability be dealing with other real estate associations who are owners of that MLS. This will require nurturing your relationships with those organizations prior to any expansion. One way of doing this is to monitor the activities of other MLSs to find any service gaps that you might fill before complete integration. As with your own MLS, other systems are looking for state-of-the-art (or better) products and services to provide for end users in ways that can enhance their business.

The ability of an MLS to leverage its size to provide end users with the best products at the best price is one of the best reasons for expansion and makes that MLS attractive as both an acquirer and an acquired. While you would do so even if expansion were not a question, maintain current information on best products, survey technical specialists within the end-user base (and elsewhere) to develop information and ideas, and communicate to end users the ideas for change that you are currently considering.

Growth can occur successfully only if you have the capacity to handle it smoothly. An MLS needs to increase its ability to accommodate growth. This has two aspects. Technically, it first needs to increase the scalability of the system. While this becomes easier as the technology improves, it must be provided for and tested before the system is opened to a larger number of users. Second, and perhaps more challenging, the internal operations of the MLS need to be able to accommodate more users. This means, among other things, more administrative personnel and more help desk capacity. In short, before growing, the MLS needs to develop a human resource plan to accommodate growth. What skill sets does the MLS need? How will it acquire them? How will it train them? These are all questions that must be answered prior to geographic expansion.

Develop a Deeper Market

Deepen your market by capturing an increased share of your customers' business. Besides operating in a wider geographic area, a second expansion strategy is to increase the number of products you provide to your customers. This goes back to the original notion of reconceiving the MLS as a technology provider. It involves the creation of tools that will enable your subscribers to be successful in the new economy.

There are a variety of areas in which this deepening can take place. To begin with, the transaction-management prize is still up for grabs. No one has yet come up with the total solution, and more important, no one has designed the way in which to integrate the systems that are being used by real estate professionals.

Consider two staples of consumer electronics, the sound system and the desktop computer. I have the option of buying all the components of either system in one package from a single manufacturer or dealer or buying components separately from different manufacturers and plugging them together to customize my system. That is not possible with a real estate transaction-management system, nor is any company working to that end. Yet, real estate firms and real estate practitioners are currently investing in pieces of technology that they would be loath to abandon and would like to plug together into a full system.

Doing any of this requires that the correct competencies and resources be available to the MLS. For most, this means increasing the resources dedicated to research and development. That is done only if the MLS and its directors view it as a technology company. Deepening the products and services offered to the original subscriber base increases the possibilities of serving a broader base because any innovations that are of benefit in the base area will benefit all practitioners and will thus find a market elsewhere.

The process begins with a market scan. Are there other industries that will pay for information and data products developed in the MLS? Marketing efforts in virtually all areas of retail sales and financial services banking rely heavily on household demographic and financial information. That information is precisely what MLSs possess in their closed sale data and their public record information. The data become even more valuable when expanded to include other public databases. So the first step is to develop parameters of potential markets, products, and revenue distribution.

The second stage of the process is to elicit shareholder input in developing the plan. It could be reasonably argued that the repurposing of MLS data to develop products for sale to other industries is a deviation from the core purpose of the organization and thus would require a solid discussion of and approval by the directors of the MLS. Involving shareholders at an early stage will preclude a great many headaches later on.

Any use of the data generated at the MLS will require clarity of ownership and right of use. That will likely mean the need to redesign data (public record) ownership structure. Currently, the reuse rights for this by the MLS are limited. Before new data products can be developed by the MLS, the use rights need to be clarified, expanded, and made more flexible.

Develop a Primary Leadership Role

Any MLS that wants to be regarded as a technology company must strive to be known as a leader in the field. This is necessary to counteract the conventional wisdom that holds that MLSs are information companies, simple repositories of real estate listings. The fastest way to this end is to become the expert organization in emerging technologies in real estate information development and distribution.

The first step here involves creating strong relationships with technology providers. The normal state of relations between MLSs and vendor companies has been that of antagonism, with each mistrusting the other and attempting to get the upper hand in any deals struck. The new economy demands that these relationships change to cooperation. MLSs have the customer bases and the basic information that will create value in the marketplace. The technology companies have the expertise to convert the information into product that will generate market share.

Alliances with technology companies will position MLSs to develop and market consulting services to peer and related organizations and create a reputation as expert advisors on issues of information and information technology. This does two things for the new MLS model. First, it opens up new markets for new product. The traditional MLS set of products was confined to information organization and connectivity among subscribers. In a new economic model, these products may remain, but they will be augmented by products developed by leveraging data and technology expertise.

Second, the image and identity of the MLS as a provider of technology tools to the real estate industry will be established and enhanced if the MLS adds technology products to the data products it has already introduced. Simply announcing a new identity is insufficient. The introduction of new products that add value to the marketplace is a clear sign of having arrived.

Having entered the market with new products, the next is to deepen the technological competency and further add value to members and subscribers by maintaining an up-to-date and complete knowledge base on relevant technology issues. This will position the MLS as the key player in the technology needs of the industry.

The sum total of this model is to re-create the traditional MLS as a technology company that offers an array of business solutions for its base constituency by combining its internal expertise with that of strategic partners. The model encompasses the creation of data products for external customers, thus increasing the equity held by MLS shareholders and increasing the size of its market. The most important part of the model is that it is scalable. Any of the products developed will benefit the core market and can be justified solely from that perspective. But they can also benefit a much broader group of users and thus extend the reach of the MLS.

A FINAL WORD: A NATIONAL MLS?

The model described above suggests a steadily declining number of MLSs. I think this is another feature of the future. The best and the brightest of the current MLSs will seize the opportunities that the market presents and will compete (successfully) with companies like Home Store, Microsoft, and Interrealty, which are also introducing new technology products into the industry. In the process, those MLSs will steadily absorb other, smaller companies. This could result in the creation of a national MLS.

More likely, however, is the success of the currently developing coalition of large MLSs. This group, formed with the help of

NAR and Home Store, is attempting to unite MLSs behind a common standard and commission the technology products needed by the coalition members' subscribers. The coalition has sufficient size and market power to set standards of data treatment and transmission and will bring the rest of the industry along. Taken together, coalition members are sufficiently big to challenge the public companies that are competing for the business of the real estate industry. Added to this is the "share of mind" now enjoyed by MLSs. These are companies to which real estate professionals have looked for years; they will automatically have the edge in any market where they can compete. If the consortium succeeds in its aim to tie the existing MLSs together, it will prevail in the market and be the de facto national MLS.

So, to come full circle to the question with which this chapter began, there is indeed a role for the MLS. But like the real estate industry, which can no longer rely on old business models, the MLS must shift as well. In real estate the old intermediary function has been eliminated by technological change, and the successful business will be forced to shift the middle and find new ways of creating value. For the MLS, the simple provision of information is not enough to sustain a business anymore. Rather, MLSs need to evolve into technology companies that succeed in the market because they understand the needs of their customers, the real estate industry, and can serve them with the tools and processes that will allow them to succeed in the new economy.

Chapter 10

Putting It All Together

We looked at many elements of business in this book. Basically, the new economy has placed new demands on business and requires change as a response. The real challenge is boiling down all these ideas and putting them into practice. Is there a small list of guidelines to follow that can position the company or the individual for success in this new economy? In this chapter, we attempt to do just this. If all the ideas presented in the previous chapters can be condensed, they would contain three ideas:

1. Be prepared to change constantly.
2. Look for your customers everywhere.
3. Deliver extraordinary customer service.

These three rules take all the detail we've developed in the previous chapters about the four businesses of real estate and create the framework you need to succeed in the new economy.

THE END IS *NOT* NEAR!

The new economy is one where technology, public policy, consumer empowerment, and globalization have combined to unleash rapid and sometimes bewildering change on American business and the real estate industry. We would all like nothing better than to see some end point, the time when change will end, when there will no longer be the constant pressure to change the way we do business. Don't count on it. The new economy is not finished yet. It will continue to evolve and business will continue to become more complicated.

The new economy gives out opportunities, not guarantees. Those opportunities are constantly shifting through new product and service markets. The successful businesses in the new economy will be alert to the emergence of new trends and profit from them. Capturing these opportunities requires the flexibility and speed to be in the right place at the right time with the right skills.

You need to introduce a nimbleness into your business. Traditionally, businesses have been all about structure and hierarchy. In the new economy, those concepts stand in the way of success. If you reread Chapter 4, you'll see the need to define your key competencies and build the business around them. Everything else can and should be discarded or outsourced. Top-producing agents understand this latter concept. They've built teams that allow for the delegation of responsibility and the specialization of labor (see Chapter 7).

The bigger challenge, however, is to redefine yourself around a set of competencies. Think about how you define your work role. The odds are that your mind is saying things like "I'm a real estate broker," "I'm a real estate agent," or "I'm an association executive." That's an old-economy mind-set. Contrast those statements with "I'm a highly organized promotions wizard who right now is applying those competencies in the real estate industry." That's a new-economy formulation.

The value of envisioning yourself or your company as a bundle of competencies is that it allows you to seize on the opportunities the new economy offers. If you see your company as a real estate company, you'll never make the move to acquire a commercial bank when the regulators demolish the existing barriers. And a great many agents entered real estate as a second career; why should it be their last? The competencies that have brought success in the agent business can be applied elsewhere.

The key here is to understand that anticipating the precise elements of change is wrong: nothing ever happens the way we think it will. Rather, understanding that change will occur and positioning your business to profit from it is the name of the game.

LOOK FOR YOUR CUSTOMERS EVERYWHERE

Recently, I was at a REALTOR® dinner in South Florida and found myself sitting next to a woman of French origin whose entire practice consisted of representing European buyers in the United States. Her business was generated through her Web site, which was in French. Her customers were initially interested in Florida but also worked with her in other U.S. markets. The Internet had put her in contact with customers; lower tax rates and a more beneficial tax treatment of real estate attracted them to American property. The interesting thing about this whole arrangement is that she is far from unique; cross-national transactions are a growing aspect of the market. Technology and globalization, two of the keys to the new economy, make this so.

Of particular concern, in light of the tragic and difficult autumn of 2001, is the prospect of continued globalization of the economy. The worldwide recession that has been around since the end of 1998 has caused the U.S. trade deficit to balloon and ultimately dragged down the domestic economy. Yet our very dependence on foreign economies is a key feature of the new economy and will be with every American industry for the foreseeable future. In real estate, this means the emergence of new customers from very different sources.

Real estate is no longer solely a domestic industry in any of its businesses. Information and transactions flow across national boundaries, bringing the MLS, brokers, and agents into the process. Associations are finding more and more areas of common ground and are fast developing an international web of real estate trade groups. In short, the industry that is organized around geography is increasingly location-free.

This represents a major change in the conventional wisdom of real estate. Traditionally, all the businesses of real estate were parochial to the extreme. Local associations had specifically defined boundaries that were tied to the street location. Agents farmed specific subareas of their markets, and even brokerages served particular markets, expanding as necessary the geographic edges of their home territories.

With globalization and technology, these boundaries are shattered. Now, customers can come from everywhere and, more important, so can competition. The use of the Internet to attract customers and the ease of information transfer opens up markets not only nationally but also globally. It allows agents and brokers to range much farther in their search for clients and customers and it allows MLSs and associations to serve market areas far beyond their traditional boundaries.

The path to success here is not paved with technology, nor does it require an international presence. Rather, success is contingent on running your business with a mind-set that defines the world as your customer base and then proceeds to narrow that base into a market of effective business relationships. Determine the competencies you possess and the manner in which you will apply them in the marketplace. This will yield a set of products and services that can constitute your market offerings. Then consider how you can make these offerings known to the widest possible set of consumers.

This process will guide you in your choice of the tools that are most useful to you. The set may or may not include a heavy dose of business and personal technology; your net may be cast across many boundaries or remain as local as the old economy. But in any case, you will be clear about what you're doing and will be alert to the possibilities of the new economy.

DON'T GIVE YOUR CUSTOMERS
ANY REASON TO LEAVE YOU

In the new economy, the consumer determines what happens in the market. The practical importance of this is that firms that do not offer either superb customer service or the absolute best product are constantly vulnerable to becoming the second choice or worse in the marketplace. Because a firm's chances of having the absolute best product are rare, every business must concentrate on service to succeed in the new economy.

As we discussed in previous chapters, world-class service revolves around meeting the needs of consumers, as the consumer visualizes those needs. The provision of world-class service, then, is a two-part task (1) understanding how consumers define their market needs and (2) meeting those needs. Both have to be part of the competencies applied by the successful new economy enterprise.

Understanding how to create value as the consumer defines value can be done in several ways. In the case where the enterprise has an effectively unlimited resource base (as in the case of the Ritz Carlton), simply empowering employees to meet every customer request and then making this part of the job description will suffice. Where that is not the case, some form of research is called for. This may involve a formal arrangement with a research organization that can do survey work or an informal testing of customer opinion through a variety of feedback mechanisms, including hearsay. The best way to understand what your customers value is just to ask them. Your business must be set up to listen to its customers.

But who are these customers? One of the major debates that has raged through the real estate industry is the one over the identity of customers. This has been particularly intense in the association business, but has affected the MLS and the broker business as well. The agent business has been largely spared the argument because their customers are clearly identified with the homebuying and homeselling public. The question is an important one because understanding the needs of the customer requires picking the right target.

Generally, the target customers for each of the businesses can be characterized as:

- brokers: primarily the public and secondarily the agents;
- MLSs: primarily the subscriber and secondarily the ownership;
- associations: primarily broker-owners and secondarily agents;
- agents: the buying and selling public.

This again differs from conventional wisdom in that it seems to minimize the position of the agent. This is not the case.

Rather, this categorization focuses on the most direct *recipients* of the services offered by each business in order to point out exactly whose needs are to be filled.

Understanding the needs of the customer is only one half the challenge, however. To be a successful new-economy business, you need to implement excellent customer service. More broadly, you need to create for your customers an experience that fully meets their needs and delivers value. This entails setting standards for the service delivered by your staff.

For the agent, the MLSs and association businesses, this is a straightforward but not necessarily easy process. In the early 1990s, we introduced standards of service and behavior at NAR. The process took about 18 months, even with the help of professional trainers. The process included education, training, and the creation of systems designed to monitor the actual performance of the staff. All these elements were crucial because creating behavioral expectations can be successful only if your people know what's to be done and if you inspect their execution of these standards. Yet, as long as this process took, it was well worth it. You simply cannot deliver an excellent customer experience without expending time and effort in creating it.

In the brokerage business this is more difficult, owing to the independence of the labor force. Agents cannot be held accountable for behavior in the same way that employees can. The key for the broker (short of moving to a salaried work force) is recruitment. If the company can establish a true brand in the market, i.e., an identifiable consistent consumer experience, it can recruit agents who understand and will work to the brand identity. This may mean a smaller and more select group of agents, but the results—extraordinary customer service and new—economy success-are worth it.

DON'T JUMP THE SHARK

There's a popular urban myth about the decline of quality in TV shows. It originates with the *Happy Days* episode in which Fonzie jumps his motorcycle over a shark during a trip to Hawaii. After that episode, it was all downhill for the show. There are now Web sites devoted to pinpointing where different programs "jumped the shark," and the debates are lively.

In all the change that the new economy engenders, you need to be careful about jumping the shark. You have, over many years, built a practice or an organization whose identity is fairly well defined in the minds of your customers. Radical change exposes you to the danger that all your work will be undone, either immediately or gradually. You will have jumped the shark.

Change is inevitable and it is good. But there is no hard rule as to how much change is enough and how fast it should occur. It is an art rather than a science. In this book, I have emphasized the need to position yourself and your business to profit both from change and from the new economy. The message has been to be aware and to be ready, but not to jump at every new thing. As quoted earlier, John Wooden told his UCLA basketball teams to "Be quick, but don't hurry." That sums up how you ought to regard change. And, as they say in Las Vegas, "Good luck!"

Index

X–Z

Broker pays to launch listing on MLS
MLS members can pull data
  to lead generation system & sell
back (referral fee) to originating
broker.